Teacher Research

Teacher Research

Stories of Learning and Growing

Deborah Roberts, Claire Bove,
and Emily van Zee, Editors

NATIONAL SCIENCE TEACHERS ASSOCIATION

Claire Reinburg, Director
Judy Cusick, Senior Editor
Andrew Cocke, Associate Editor
Betty Smith, Associate Editor
Robin Allan, Book Acquisitions Coordinator

Art and Design Will Thomas, Director
   Will Thomas, Cover Art and Inside Design

Printing and Production Catherine Lorrain, Director
   Nguyet Tran, Assistant Production Manager
   Jack Parker, Electronic Prepress Technician

National Science Teachers Association
Gerald F. Wheeler, Executive Director
David Beacom, Publisher

Library of Congress Cataloging-in-Publication Data

Teacher research : stories of learning and growing / Deborah Roberts, Claire Bove, and Emily van Zee, editors.
   p. cm.
 ISBN 978-1-933531-13-7
 1. Action research in education--United States. 2. Education--Research--United States. I. Roberts,
Deborah. II. Bove, Claire. III. Zee, Emily van.
LB1028.24.T39 2007
370.7'2--dc22
                     2007011123

Contents

Engaging Teachers in Research on Science Learning and Teaching
Emily H. van Zee and Deborah Roberts

Part One Integrating Science and Literacy Learning

Chapter 1
How Can Playing With a Motion Detector Help Children Learn to Write
Kathleen Dillon Hogan

Chapter 2
Reading, Writing, Comprehension, and Confidence—Achieved in Science
Elizabeth Kline

Chapter 3
Trisha Kagey Boswell

Chapter 4
Monica Hartman

Part Two Ongoing Studies of Learning and Teaching in Science Contexts

Chapter 5
Ellen Franz

Part Three **Reflections on Researching While Teaching**

Foreword

I am honored to be invited to write the foreword for this book. I always consider it a privilege to be allowed into the classrooms of teachers, and that is what this book does for its readers. Learning is a complex process, and the learning environments of homes, neighborhoods, museums, classrooms, and such add to the complexity. When teachers share the results of their inquiry into their practice, especially into their own thinking or that of their students as they do in this book, we are able to add to our own experience as learners and teachers.

What is teacher research? It usually starts with wondering about some aspect of teaching or learning that comes from the phenomena of the classroom. As the chapters in this book suggest, the catalyst for the wondering may have come from looking at student artifacts or at some sort of data that relates to student performance. Other aspects of research often included in teacher research are collecting information, designing an intervention, predicting effects or hypothesizing what and why change will happen, formulating questions amenable to research, analyzing data to obtain results and answer questions, concluding what was learned, and communicating methods, results, and conclusions. A difference that sometimes leads some people not to include teacher research as research is the level of rigor in the application of the various aspects. In the chapters that follow, you will see these aspects included at varying degrees of rigor.

Typically, teacher research also involves engineering to solve an identified problem. In my own classroom, my career as a researcher began with me wondering why my students didn't perform well on certain test items. Usually these were the items my students called "tricky." They really weren't so much tricky as they were not simply repeats of essentially the questions they had already answered during class activities. As a teacher I designed an instructional intervention that I thought would change students' understanding and then probed to see whether the intervention effected any change. Having done this teacher research, I then went on to make my research methods or approaches more specific.

Why might a teacher want to conduct research? One reason is that the teacher research may be able to answer a question of direct and immediate interest to the teacher, a question whose answer would give the teacher information about student learning or the effects of instruction. The immediate value is to the teacher. If the teacher never shares the results, the new knowledge is limited to that teacher. Another key objective for teacher research then is to share the new knowledge with others, especially other teachers. That is part of what this book does.

Teacher Research: Stories of Learning and Growing has several potential uses. It can be used by individual teachers or by teacher groups. Individual teachers can read it to become familiar with the sorts of queries other teachers have about their practice and how they went about their inquiry. Groups of teachers collaborating within a school system attempting to reform their instruction could read chapters at regular intervals and discuss their thoughts about the chapter and the possible implications it might have for teacher research around their own inquiries into teaching and learning in their collective classrooms. Teachers of teachers might have their preservice or inservice teachers read and discuss chapters as a way of stimulating their growth as professionals who think about the improvement of the practice of teaching.

As you read each chapter in this book, note the question(s) asked by the author, the data or information sources the author goes to, and the inferences the author draws from the data. Note also what adjustments to procedures, interactions with learners, or next lessons the teacher implements. It is this last step that tells us that (and what) teacher learning has resulted from the teacher research. How you change your practice as a result of reading this book will be evidence of your learning.

Jim Minstrell
FACET Innovations
Seattle, Washington

We invite you into the classrooms of the authors to get to know their students, their practices, and their experiences. What we have discovered, as these authors and others have too, is that once one experiences "doing" teacher research, one cannot let go. One question or discovery leads to another, a colleague's observation lends a different lens to view the classroom, or a conversation with a student sheds light on a multitude of issues. What we are hoping you will gain is some insight into a variety of classrooms and situations. We hope something you read piques a deep curiosity within you, a curiosity waiting to be satisfied by the understanding only you can gain by exploring your own questions. We hope you might look at your classroom in a different way, at your teaching in a different light, and at each of your students as vessels of great understanding, waiting to be understood in a way no one else has been able to understand them before.

Each teacher is unique; every classroom is different. In this collection, there are chapters by beginning teachers and chapters by very experienced teachers. There are chapters by teachers who have just begun to do research in their classrooms in an intentional way and by those who are undertaking doctoral studies. The book offers glimpses into a variety of situations, through the perspectives of a variety of individuals, and in a variety of formats.

The practice of teaching, even for teachers who do not think of themselves as researchers, is one in which the elements of research are present. Asking questions about practice, collecting evidence, making sense of the evidence, and sharing conclusions with others: These activities are happening all over schools during every school day, and they are elements of research. The job of a teacher is to facilitate student learning, not to produce and publish formal research findings, but these elements of research are embedded within facilitating student learning—sometimes as part of normal practice, sometimes as intentional acts, and sometimes as a more formal research process.

Table 1 on p. xi presents a spectrum of research practices for the elements of questioning, collecting evidence, making sense of the evidence, and sharing findings. Writing in a lesson plan book, for example, is, in our view, an act of research because a teacher briefly documents what happened and notes ideas for making changes next time. Choosing and making copies of examples of student work is an intentional act of research in which a teacher also documents student learning. A formal documentary practice would be to create an archive of lesson plans, copies of student work, tapes of instruction, and other artifacts.

The authors of this book are sharing with you the records of their research. Each of these teachers views the practice of teaching as a research activity. Some have just begun to see their practice in this way; others have long viewed their teaching practice as an act of research. We have identified what we see as the elements of each teacher's research in a box at the end of

Table 1: Elements of research

Elements of Research Embedded in Normal Teaching Practices	Intentional Research Practices	Formal Research Practices
QUESTIONING		
Noticing and wondering in the act of teaching	Generating issues to be explored Becoming aware of relevant literature	Formulating a formal research question Developing a theoretical framework within which that question will be examined
COLLECTING EVIDENCE		
Having stacks of student work	Choosing and copying examples of student writings and drawings	Audio- and videotaping instruction
Noting what happened and ideas for changes in a lesson plan book		Archiving lesson plans, student work, e-mail messages, and other artifacts
	Keeping anecdotal records of student progress	
Having students assemble portfolios of their work	Writing a reflective journal	Generating data such as responses on surveys
MAKING SENSE OF THE EVIDENCE		
Thinking about what happened Talking with colleagues	Discussing copies of student work Writing descriptive accounts of what happened Making connections to others' relevant findings	Watching and discussing video clips of students in action Writing analyses of students' actions and utterances Analyzing survey responses Writing about ways that findings support or disconfirm results reported elsewhere
SHARING		
Talking with colleagues	Meeting with a teacher inquiry group Facilitating discussion of student learning during a staff meeting	Presenting at a conference Writing for publication

each chapter. In reading our interpretation of these classroom stories, you will be able to see and identify these elements in your own practice.

The demands of classroom teaching are overwhelming. Each year, in this era of high-stakes testing, standards, and accountability, those demands increase. At the end of the year, it is easy for a teacher to feel that he or she has been insanely busy, but it is sometimes difficult for that teacher to feel a sense of having accomplished anything beyond survival. You may wonder what possible reason there could be to add teacher research to the burden.

Our answer to this excellent question is that the inquiry process—the act of asking a question, of gathering evidence, analyzing the evidence, drawing conclusions, and sharing those conclusions with others—is a way for a teacher to recognize teaching as the intellectual endeavor that it is. Inquiry is an exercise in critical thinking. It is a creative act. Even with today's top-down reforms, scripted curricula, and teacher-proof lessons, inquiry can rekindle the fire of enthusiasm that brought us to teaching and keep that fire burning as we share our enthusiasm with our students and with our colleagues.

These authors have reflected on their own science teaching and the learning of their students in ways that show their continuing efforts to push forward the reforms advocated by the *National Science Education Standards* (NRC 1996) and *Benchmarks for Science Literacy* (AAAS 1993). The *National Science Education Standards* advocates that teachers have experiences "to learn and use the skills of research to generate new knowledge about school science and the teaching and learning of science" (NRC 1996, p. 68).

Teacher educators may have expectations for teacher research that differ from some of the examples in this collection. A common approach in a master's program, for example, is to require a research course in which teachers focus on specific ways of investigating aspects of what is happening in their classrooms and schools. Reports of such research tend to be shaped by traditional formats, such as sections stating research questions, describing methods, presenting findings, and discussing what has been learned and actions taken. The perspective taken in this book represents a broader view of teacher research: What can teachers do to deepen their own understandings of their teaching practices and students' learning and to share that wisdom with other teachers? From this perspective, teacher research can be reported as a poem, story, or descriptive account of what happened as well as a formal research report.

Part One includes four examples of research in progress by teachers who wrote about aspects of integrating science and literacy learning. Part Two presents a variety of inquiries about learning and teaching in science contexts at a variety of grade levels in a variety of formats. In Part Three, the authors reflect upon the process of researching while teaching.

For us, teacher research encompasses this broad spectrum of activities and products. We invite you to join us in this enterprise!

Deborah Roberts
Claire Bove
Emily van Zee

Teacher Research

Acknowledgments

We thank our students, colleagues, mentors, administrators, and families for their support and interest in these endeavors. We also thank the Spencer Foundation Practitioner Research Mentoring and Communication program for a series of grants that made possible the inquiries of many of these authors as participants in the Science Inquiry Group facilitated by Emily van Zee while she was a faculty member at the University of Maryland, College Park. In addition, we gratefully acknowledge support by the National Science Foundation for investigations of questioning during conversations about science, under grant #MDR 91-55726. We deeply appreciate the opportunity for some of us to participate in the Carnegie Academy for the Scholarship of Teaching and Learning sponsored by the Carnegie Foundation for the Advancement of Teaching. The data presented, the statements made, and the views expressed are solely the responsibility of the authors and do not necessarily reflect the views of the foundations.

About the Editors

Deborah Roberts is a founding member of the Science Inquiry Group, whose commitment to teacher research inspired the establishment of Teacher Research Day at national NSTA (National Science Teachers Association) conferences. Now a fifth-grade teacher in Arizona, she also has served as a district and state instructional specialist for science in Maryland. Roberts earned her bachelor's degree in elementary education and her master's in science education from the University of Maryland.

Claire Bove has taught science at Bancroft Middle School in San Leandro, California, where she chaired the science department for many years. She also has served as a cooperating teacher for Mills College, a district mentor teacher, and Beginning Teacher Support and Assessment mentor. Currently she facilitates teacher professional development activities for Mills College. Bove is a graduate of the University of California at Berkeley with a bachelor's in molecular and cell biology and a master's and a credential in science and mathematics education.

Emily van Zee founded the Science Inquiry Group with funding from the Spencer Foundation. She organizes Teacher Researcher Day for national NSTA conferences. She has taught middle school science as well as introductory physics and undergraduate and graduate courses in science education at several universities. She is now an associate professor of science education at Oregon State University. She earned a bachelor's in physics from Radcliffe College and a master's in physics and a PhD in psychology from the University of Washington.

Introduction

Engaging Teachers in Research on Science Learning and Teaching*

Emily H. van Zee and Deborah Roberts

Professional Development Standard C of the National Science Education Standards recommends that professional development activities for teachers "provide opportunities to learn and use the skills of research to generate new knowledge about science and the teaching and learning of science " (NRC 1996, p. 68). This chapter considers four issues underlying this standard:

What does it mean for a teacher to be a researcher?
How do teachers inquire into science learning and teaching?
Why would they undertake such inquiries?
In what ways do they use and communicate their findings?

What Does It Mean for a Teacher to Be a Researcher?

In her essay "Teaching as Research," Eleanor Duckworth (1987) articulated the following vision:

I am not proposing that school teachers single-handedly become published researchers in the development of human learning. Rather I am proposing that teaching, understood as engaging learners in phenomena and working to understand the sense they are making, might be the sine qua non of such research.

This kind of researcher would be a teacher in the sense of caring about some part of the world and how it works enough to want to make it accessible to others. He or she would be fascinated by the questions of how to engage people in it and how people make sense of it and would have time and resources to pursue these questions to the depth of his or her interest, to write what he or she learned, and to contribute to the theoretical and pedagogical discussions on the nature and development of human learning (p. 168).

* Reprinted from Rhoton, J., and P. Shane, eds. 2006. *Teaching Science in the 21st Century.* Arlington, VA: NSTA Press.

This word *research* recognizes teachers as legitimate participants in efforts to improve instruction through explorations of questions about student learning. Such usage is controversial, however, as some prefer to reserve the word *research* for more formal investigations (Hammer and Schifter 2001; Richardson 1994).

In this chapter *research* refers to a continuum of acts associated with generating knowledge. At one end of the continuum, acts of research include a fleeting question about student thinking that emerges in the midst of a discussion: the teacher is identifying an issue that could be explored. Most teacher research involves articulating questions of interest, developing interpretations of data collected while teaching, modifying instruction in light of these interpretations, and perhaps sharing findings with colleagues. The more intentional and systematic the process, the more others perceive these efforts to be research. Acts of research at the opposite end of the continuum include reporting results at professional meetings and in refereed publications, particularly results from teachers who undertake extensive studies.

The findings of teacher research apply only to the context within which the study was conducted but may be more valid for that context than findings from studies conducted in many locations with randomized designs. Teacher research techniques can be used to examine whether findings from a formal study with generalizable results apply to a teacher's own students. Judgments of the quality of teacher research typically include trustworthiness and transferability (Lincoln and Guba 1985) rather than reliability and generalizability because the latter are rarely feasible in studies teachers conduct in their classrooms. Roth (2007) proposes "evidence-based reasoning" and "worthwhile questions" as appropriate aspects to be considered. Although findings from one study in one classroom would not be generalizable, findings from a variety of settings in which teacher-researchers have focused on an issue can be discussed in terms of their broader implications. Assertions about questioning practices, for example, have been made on the basis of a series of individual case studies (van Zee et al. 2001).

Inquiring into one's own teaching practices and students' learning also is known as the "scholarship of teaching and learning" (Hutchings 2000), "self-study" (Dinkelman 2003), "critical reflection" (Nichols et al. 1997), "classroom inquiry" (Hubbard and Power 1993, 1999), "teacher inquiry" (Hammer and Schifter 2001), "action research" (Feldman 1996), "research on practice" (Richardson 1994), and "practitioner research" (Zeichner and Noffke 2001). Such research captures the "wisdom of practice" (Shulman 2004) and contributes knowledge generated from the unique perspective of the instructor.

How Do Teachers Inquire Into
Science Learning and Teaching?

Conducting research in the midst of teaching is challenging. A good way to start is to listen closely to what students are saying (Paley 1986). Most teacher-researchers undertake qualitative studies in which they collect and interpret data such as videotapes of instruction, copies of student writings and drawings, e-mail messages, anecdotal records, reflective journals, interviews, and surveys (Cochran-Smith and Lytle 1993; Hubbard and Power 1993, 1999; Mills 2003; White and Gunstone 1992). Descriptive statistics and other quantitative methods also can be used effectively (McLean 1995).

An Example

An article published in a journal for teachers, *Science and Children,* provides an example of teacher research. In "Kids Questioning Kids: Experts Sharing," Marletta Iwasyk wrote about ways in which her first-grade students asked questions of one another during conversations about light and shadows (1997). She stated the issue she was exploring, described how she conducted the research, included information about the curricular context, provided a transcript as example data, and shared her interpretations as follows:

> I believe that children are capable of being teachers and while engaged in the teaching process, they reinforce and solidify their own learning.... To examine how this happens in my classroom, I conducted a case study.... The case study involved analysis of transcripts of students discussing the subject of shadows in which two students became the "teachers" or "leaders" and the rest asked questions for clarification or gave input of their own.
>
> To document the discussions, I used a tape recorder with a microphone placed on a desk near the seated children. I also placed a video camera high in an unobtrusive corner. The camera was trained on the seats in the middle of the circle where I placed the "leaders" of the discussion. If other students had something to contribute, I asked them to step to the middle of the circle where I knew they would be visible to the camera....
>
> On the very first sunny day of school in the fall, we begin our study of shadows.... The sidebar lists some suggestions for various shadow activities.... Many questions arise.... In the beginning I do not answer any of the questions; instead, I ask the children to think about the questions and discover how they can find the answers for themselves. If they make early conclusions about what they observe, I do not acknowledge any answer as right or wrong....

Teacher Research

See *Student Conversations* [in a box on a page] for an example of dialog that took place during a discussion of shadows…. One of the questions asked and discussed was "Why doesn't it [the shadow] have the color you have on?" This student wondered why the shadow wasn't the same color as skin…. Just as questions can help children clarify their own thinking, the teacher can learn much about the students by listening to their discussions. It was very enlightening for me to observe thinking processes as the children gave explanations … (1997, pp. 42–46).

Iwasyk's case study adds to the literature an example of inquiry learning and teaching within a specific context. The children's questions illustrate unexpected ideas that teachers are likely to hear if they encourage students to talk about what they think. Iwasyk developed this case study while participating in a teacher-researcher group exploring student and teacher questioning during conversations about science (van Zee et al. 2001).

Experiences in a Teacher-Researcher Group

Participants in teacher-researcher groups support one another as they explore their own questions about learning and teaching. In her book *Talking Their Way Into Science: Hearing Children's Questions and Theories, Responding With Curricula*, Karen Gallas, a first- and second-grade teacher, described the process as follows:

My research on Science Talks began in 1989 when I first joined the Brookline Teacher Research Seminar. At that time I started to tape and transcribe Science Talks, and with the help of seminar members began to try and make sense of them. In the early stages of this work, Sarah Michaels [faculty member at Clark University] was extremely helpful to me, both because she encouraged me to pursue my interest and because she showed me how to look at complex data in a thoughtful and open way. Since then, the members of the seminar have continued to be interested and creative in their responses to the many transcripts I have shared. Their dedication to understanding children's intentions and meanings is always a source of support and inspiration (1995, p. vii).

Role of University Researchers

The role of university researchers in facilitating teacher-researcher groups differs substantially from the role of university researchers in initiating research projects in schools. In the latter projects, university researchers typically generate the questions explored, design the strategies or curricula that participating teachers try to implement, interpret data collected in the teachers' classrooms without involving the teachers in these analyses, and refer to participating teachers with pseudonyms, if at all, in publishing findings. In contrast, the role of university researchers in facilitating teacher-researcher groups is to foster the *teachers'* inquiries through organizing meetings, gathering resources, and supporting the teachers as the teachers generate issues, design ways to explore those issues, collect data, develop interpretations of their data, and present findings. Although the focus of the group may reflect the university researcher's interests (e.g., Michaels and Sohmer 2005), the teachers undertake their own studies and author or coauthor reports of their findings.

Support From School Administrators

The importance of school administrators in fostering teacher research was acknowledged by the teachers (Patty Jacobs and Caryn McCrohon) and university researchers (Maureen Reddy and Leslie Herrenkohl) who were co-authors of the book *Creating Scientific Communities in the Elementary Classroom*:

> We have also been helped by a number of other people whom we would like to thank. Five years ago, Joan Merrill, with characteristic foresight, recognized the potential of our collaboration. As principal of the Goddard School of Science and Technology, she often speaks about "inviting children into learning." Her belief that a school can be a community of inquiry, for adults and children alike, has also invited us into learning (Reddy et al. 1998, p. ix).

Such administrative support may include arranging schedules so teacher-researchers can meet regularly, providing a place to meet and resources, promoting an environment where teachers are motivated to undertake in-depth looks at their students' learning, using the findings to guide school decision making and long-range planning, and encouraging dissemination of results.

Districtwide Initiatives

Some school districts have started teacher-research groups facilitated by school district personnel. The Fairfax County, Virginia, public schools, for example, undertook a concerted effort to improve instruction through teacher research (Mohr et al. 2003). Not only did the district sustain a network of teacher-researchers over many years, but it also sponsored a regional teacher-researcher conference each spring at which participating teachers presented their studies. In the book *Teacher Research for Better Schools*, the authors offer recommendations for teacher colleagues, school-level administrators, central office administrators, teacher educators, professional developers, parents, and school communities.

Teacher Research

Teacher Research in Preparation and Professional Development

Pekarek, Krockover, and Shephardson recommended that "the notion of teachers as researchers ought to be incorporated in science teacher preparation and professional development programs" (1996, p. 112). One approach is to reconceptualize science teaching methods courses with a reflection orientation (Abell and Bryan 1997). Another is to engage prospective teachers in inquiries into science learning and teaching, particularly if these can be in collaboration with practicing teacher-researchers (van Zee 1998; van Zee et al. 2003).

High-quality professional development programs engage teachers in long-term learning about science and about learning and teaching (Stiles and Mundry 2002). An example is described by Wendy Saul, who collaborated with teachers on a project to integrate science and literacy. Some of the participating teachers became authors of chapters in several books. In *Science Workshop: Reading, Writing, and Thinking Like a Scientist*, Saul reflected upon the teachers' learning experiences as follows:

> [The coauthors] are teachers whose classrooms have changed not as a result of a new curriculum package but because of intense professional discussions and extensive reading. They have learned from and with colleagues whose insights and questions made the strange familiar and the familiar strange. They have explored, investigated, and analyzed scientific phenomena themselves so that they could understand what children engaged in schoolwork need to think about and feel and understand. The public recital of their experiences represents a commitment not only to a workshop model, but to a profession that values intelligence, community, and caring (2002, pp. 15–16).

One of the participants, Charles Pearce (1999), wrote a book, *Nurturing Inquiry: Real Science for the Elementary Classroom*. It provides a detailed account of how he gets started and sustains inquiry throughout the year in his fifth-grade classroom.

Why Would Teachers Undertake Inquiries Into Science Learning and Teaching?

Primary motivations for undertaking teacher research include the learning that occurs as well as the satisfaction of sharing new understandings with others. A kindergarten teacher, Vivian Paley, reflected on the difference between participating in a researcher's study and undertaking her own studies as follows:

Until I had my own questions to ask, my own set of events to watch, and my own ways of combining all of these with teaching, I did not learn very much at all ... I have studied the subject [of children's play] through teaching and writing, and I cannot do one without the other. For me, the tape recorder is a necessity. I transcribe each day's play and stories and conversations and then make up my own stories about what is happening.... [The children's] fantasies propelled me further into surprises and mysteries, and I hungered after better ways to report what I heard and saw, and to find out what it all had to do with teaching (Paley and Coles 1999, pp. 16, 18, 20).

Another motivation is the desire to design effective instruction that addresses one's commitments. In *Connecting Girls to Science: Constructivism, Feminism, and Science Education Reform,* for example, Elaine Howes wrote about her high school biology study:

Listening to students is pedagogically consistent with my feminist commitments and with my desire to create and study instruction that attends to "science for all." This study of contexts in which I tried—and succeeded to differing degrees—to really hear what these students were saying forms the core of this book. While I concentrate on students' ideas and beliefs, I also include my reflections on their ideas and how these might inform instructional and curricular choices. Thus this teacher-research project originated in my commitments, which led to the development of specific instructional contexts, which in turn allowed me to hear students' voices in ways that are typically absent in traditional instruction (2002, p. 5).

Teachers who systematically analyze their students' learning and own teaching practices contribute to the knowledge base and help bring into view questions that need to be asked. Detailed accounts of what individual instructors consider inquiry learning and teaching to be, for example, can provide an empirical base upon which to build a deeper understanding of what "learning science through inquiry" means. The potential of engaging teachers in this way was recognized many decades ago by John Dewey, who wrote in *Progressive Education and the Science of Education:*

The method of the teacher ... becomes a matter of finding the conditions, which call out self-educative activity, or learning, and of cooperating with the activities of the pupils so that they have learning as their consequence.... A series of constantly multiplying careful reports on conditions which experience has shown in actual cases to be favorable or unfavorable to learning would revolutionize the whole subject of method (1928/1959, pp. 125–126).

Teacher Research

Generating knowledge through such case studies is a feasible way for teachers to contribute to the research enterprise. For example, Roberts (1999) reported on ways parents became involved when she asked her students to watch the Moon. Simpson (1997) reflected on ways she engaged students in collaborative dialogues. Phyllis Whitin, with assistance from David Whitin, recorded her students' year-long exploration of bird behaviors in *Inquiry at the Window: Pursuing the Wonders of Learners* (1997). Another teacher author, Ellen Doris (1991), included transcripts of dialogues, copies of students' writings and drawings, and photos in documenting her students' inquiries in *Doing What Scientists Do: Children Learn to Investigate Their World*. When serving as texts or supplements in courses for teachers, such journal articles and books ground discussions of inquiry learning and teaching in specific contexts.

In What Ways Do Teachers Use and Communicate Their Findings?

Teacher-researchers use their findings in ongoing efforts to improve instruction. For example, in "Conceptual Development Research in the Natural Setting of a Secondary School Science Classroom," Jim Minstrell, a high school physics teacher, described his use of data to inform his teaching practices:

> The initiative for my research in alternative conceptions grew out of the frustrations of my own teaching experiences, particularly the frustration that my very rational (to me) instructional activities were less effective than I desired .... Data for this study were gathered in the context of the activities in [two] physics classes. Typically, prior to studying a new unit, a pre-instruction quiz was administered to determine the extent to which students were using alternative conceptions. They were usually paper-and-pencil quizzes and included questions designed to be sensitive to alternative conceptual structures. Some questions were adapted from those used by other researchers ... other questions were developed based on difficulties identified in my classes in earlier years. Other data on alternative initial conceptions came from tape recordings of large- or small-group discussions within the classes. I monitored the tenacity of the alternative conceptions, as would any teacher, by paying careful attention to what they said in discussions, wrote in lab reports, and did on tests that I constructed (1982, p. 131).

Minstrell communicated his findings in presentations at professional meetings and in publications for teachers and researchers (2001; Minstrell and Kraus 2005). By applying for grants, he obtained funding for release time to conduct his research more systematically than would have been otherwise possible.

The funding enabled him to create a community of teacher-researchers within his school as he coached two mathematics teachers to use his approach to teach several of his physics classes. He also invited university researchers to join him, his colleagues, and his students in investigating physics learning. This enabled him to draw on university resources to accomplish some of his research goals. Building on his ongoing studies, Minstrell constructed a system of "facets of knowledge" that guided his design of instruction and assessments in many physical science contexts (2001). These facets formed the bases for computer diagnostic programs that students could use to check their understandings, now available free as tools for assessment at *www.Diagnoser.com*.

Teacher-researchers communicate their findings in a variety of ways. These may include talking informally with their grade-level team members, leading discussions at school faculty meetings, and presenting districtwide workshops on the issues they are exploring. They also may present their findings at local conferences for teacher-researchers and at national meetings such as Teacher-Researcher Day at National Science Teachers Association (NSTA) conferences. They may publish their findings in school district or state organization newsletters, journals for teachers, discipline-specific journals, research journals, and books.

Teacher-researchers also may contribute to the public conversation about learning and teaching by developing documentary websites that enable anyone with internet access to explore their experiences and perspectives on issues they have formulated and examined. The Carnegie Foundation for the Advancement of Teaching, for example, has mounted a "Gallery of Teaching and Learning" with "snapshots of practice" that K–12 and higher education Carnegie Scholars have developed. Emily Wolk's snapshot documents the participatory action research that she undertook with elementary students to examine and modify a dangerous intersection near her school (*http://gallery.carnegiefoundation.org/ewolk*). Denis Jacobs, a college chemistry professor, developed a snapshot that presented an alternative approach to general chemistry in which he addressed the needs of at-risk students with cooperative learning strategies (*http://gallery.carnegiefoundation.org/djacobs*). Deborah Smith, a science teacher educator, documented ways in which she engaged science-phobic preservice teachers in her course on methods of teaching science in elementary school (*http://gallery.carnegiefoundation.org/collections/castl_he/dsmith*). Teacher-researchers interested in developing their own web-based snapshots of practice can use the foundation's freely available KEEP (Knowledge, Exchange, Exhibition, Presentation) Toolkit to communicate their studies to others (at *www.cfkeep.org*).

Reflection

Teachers act as researchers every day as they listen closely to their students, consider what to do next, how and why, and pause to wonder about some aspect of what is happening in their classrooms. Those who undertake systematic studies contribute to the research enterprise when they make their findings public through workshops, presentations, and publications. University researchers can foster teacher research by supporting teachers in their inquiries. School administrators can create environments in which teachers are motivated to take an in-depth look at teaching and learning in their classrooms. Thus teacher research has the potential to improve instruction directly by engaging teachers in seeking to understand deeply how their students learn. Teacher research also has the potential to influence science teaching practices through generation of findings that are credible to other teachers in the field.

Emily H. van Zee [when this chapter originally appeared]

is an associate professor of science education at the University of Maryland, College Park. She collaborates with teachers in development of case studies of science learning and teaching. She is a Carnegie Scholar in teacher education and participant in the Carnegie Academy for the Scholarship of Teaching and Learning.

Deborah Roberts [when this chapter originally appeared]

is the instructional specialist in elementary science for the Montgomery County Public Schools, Maryland. She engages teachers in research as part of the Howard Hughes Student Inquiry Project. She is a K–12 Carnegie Scholar and participant in the Carnegie Academy for the Scholarship of Teaching and Learning.

References

Abell, S. K., and L. A. Bryan. 1997. Reconceptualizing the elementary science methods course using a reflection orientation. *Journal of Science Teacher Education* 8: 153–166.

Cochran-Smith, M., and S. Lytle. 1993. *Inside/outside: Teacher research and knowledge.* New York: Teachers College Press.

Dewey, J. 1928/1959. Progressive education and the science of education. In *Dewey on education selections.* M. S. Dworkin, ed. 113–126. New York: Teachers College Press.

Dinkelman, T. 2003. Self-study in teacher education: A means and ends tool for promoting reflective teaching. *Journal of Teacher Education* 54 (1): 6–18.

Doris, E. 1991. *Doing what scientists do: Children learn to investigate their world.* Portsmouth, NH: Heinemann.

Duckworth, E. 1987. *The having of wonderful ideas and other essays on teaching and learning.* New York: Teachers College Press.

Feldman, A. 1996. Enhancing the practice of physics teachers: Mechanisms for the generation and sharing of knowledge and understanding in collaborative action research. *Journal of Research in Science Teaching* 33: 512–540.

Gallas, K. 1995. *Talking their way into science: Hearing children's questions and theories, responding with curricula.* New York: Teachers College Press.

Hammer, D., and D. Schifter. 2001. Practices of inquiry in teaching and research. *Cognition and Instruction* 19 (4): 441–78.

Howes, E. 2002. *Connecting girls and science: Constructivism, feminism, and science education reform*. New York: Teachers College Press.

Hubbard, R. S., and B. M. Power. 1993. *The art of classroom inquiry: A handbook for teacher research*. Portsmouth, NH: Heinemann.

Hubbard, R. S., and B. M. Power. 1999. *Living the questions: A guide for teacher-researchers*. York, ME: Stenhouse.

Hutchings, P. 2000. *Opening lines: Approaches to the scholarship of teaching and learning*. Palo Alto, CA: Carnegie Foundation for the Advancement of Teaching.

Iwasyk, M. 1997. Kids questioning kids: "Experts" sharing. *Science and Children* 35 (1): 42–46.

Lincoln, Y., and E. Guba. 1985. Emerging criteria for quality in qualitative and interpretive research. *Qualitative Inquiry* 1 (3): 275–289.

McLean, J. E. 1995. *Improving education through action research: A guide for administrators and teachers*. Thousand Oaks, CA: Corwin Press.

Michaels, S., and R. Sohmer. 2005. The "two puppies" story: The role of narrative in teaching and learning science. In *Narrative interaction*. U. Quasthoff and T. Becker, eds., 57–91. Amsterdam: Benjamins.

Mills, G. 2003. *Action research: A guide for the teacher-researcher*. 2nd ed. NJ: Merrill.

Minstrell, J. 1982. Conceptual development research in the natural setting of the classroom. In *Education for the 80's: Science*, ed. M. B. Rowe, 129–143. Washington, DC: National Education Association.

Minstrell, J. 2001. Facets of students' thinking: Designing to cross the gap from research to standards-based practice. In *Designing for science: Implications for everyday, classroom and professional settings*. eds. K. Crowley, C. D. Schunn, and T. Okada, 415–444. Mahwah, NJ: Lawrence Erlbaum.

Minstrell, J., and P. Kraus. 2005. Guided inquiry in the science classroom. In *How students learn: History, mathematics, and science in the classroom*, eds. M.S. Donovan and J. D. Bransford, 475–524. Washington, DC: National Academy Press.

Mohr, M. M., C. Rogers, B. Sanford, M. A. Nocerino, M. MacLean, S. Clawson, and A. Lieberman. 2003. *Teacher research for better schools*. New York: Teachers College Press.

National Research Council (NRC). 1996. *National Science Education Standards*. Washington, DC: National Academy Press.

Nichols, S. E., D. Tippins, and K. Wieseman. 1997. A "toolkit" for developing critically reflective science teachers. *Research in Science Education* 27 (2): 175–94.

Paley, V. 1986. On listening to what the children say. *Harvard Educational Review* 56 (2): 122–131.

Paley, V., and R. Coles. 1999. *The boy who would be a helicopter*. Cambridge, MA: Harvard University Press.

Pearce, C. 1999. *Nurturing inquiry*. Portsmouth, NH: Heinemann.

Pekarek, R., G. H. Krockover, and D. P. Shephardson. 1996. The research-practice gap in science education. *Journal of Research in Science Teaching* 33: 111–114.

Reddy, M., P. Jacobs, C. McCrohon, and L. R. Herrenkohl. 1998. *Creating scientific communities in the elementary classroom*. Portsmouth, NH: Heinemann.

Richardson, V. 1994. Conducting research on practice. *Educational Researcher* 23 (5): 5–10.

Roberts, D. 1999. The sky's the limit: Parents and first-grade students observe the sky. *Science and Children* 37: 33–37.

Roth, K. 2007. Science teachers as researchers. In *Handbook of research on science education*. S. K. Abell and N. G. Lederman, eds. Mahwah, NJ: Erlbaum.

Saul, W., J. Reardon, C. Pearce, D. Dieckman, and D. Neutze. 2002. *Science workshop: Reading, writing, and thinking like a scientist*. 2nd ed. Portsmouth, NH: Heinemann.

Shulman, L. S. 2004. *The wisdom of practice: Essays on teaching, learning, and learning to teach*. San Francisco: Jossey-Bass.

Teacher*Research*

Simpson, D. 1997. Collaborative conversations: Strategies for engaging students in productive dialogues. *The Science Teacher* 64 (88): 40–43.

Stiles, K. E., and S. Mundry. 2002. Professional development and how teachers learn: Developing expert science teachers. In *Learning science and the science of learning*, ed. R. W. Bybee, 137–151. Arlington, VA: NSTA Press.

van Zee, E. H. 1998. Fostering elementary teachers' research on their science teaching practices. *Journal of Teacher Education* 49: 245–254.

van Zee, E. H., M. Iwasyk, A. Kurose, D. Simpson, and J. Wild. 2001. Student and teacher questioning during conversations about science. *Journal of Research in Science Teaching* 38:159–190.

van Zee, E. H., D. Lay, and D. Roberts. 2003. Fostering collaborative inquiries by prospective and practicing elementary and middle school teachers. *Science Education* 87: 588–612.

White, R., and R. Gunstone. 1992. *Probing understanding*. London: Falmer Press.

Whitin, P., and D. J. Whitin. 1997. *Inquiry at the window: Pursuing the wonders of learners*. Portsmouth, NH: Heinemann.

Zeichner, K., and S. Noffke. 2001. Practitioner research. In *Handbook of research on teaching*, 4th ed. V. Richardson, 298–330. Washington, DC: American Educational Research Association.

Integrating Science and Literacy Learning

Literacy learning includes not only learning how to read with comprehension but also learning how to write clearly, to question appropriately, to listen respectfully, and to speak effectively. This set of case studies explores integrating science and such literacy learning. These are works in progress by teachers who identified issues that interested them and collected data to inform their thinking about their students' learning. Kathleen Hogan describes how she engaged first-grade students in writing sequential directions while exploring motion. Elizabeth Kline reports on ways she engaged her fifth-grade students in integrating reading and writing in a science context. Trisha Kagey Boswell reflects upon questions her fourth-grade students asked while exploring electric circuits. In demonstrating a *science talk*, Monica Hartman tracks fifth-grade students' ideas about why they see water drops on the outside of a glass of ice.

Chapter 1

How Can Playing With a Motion Detector Help Children Learn to Write Clear Sequential Directions?

Kathleen Dillon Hogan

Kathleen Dillon Hogan is a kindergarten teacher in the Calvert County, Maryland, public schools. When this paper was written, she was a first-grade teacher at Hyattsville Elementary School in Hyattsville, Maryland. Kathleen heard a colleague describe how her first-grade students were using motion detectors and computers to learn about line graphs (see Chapter 13). She interested her school's reading specialist in trying this with her students, and together they invented a new way to teach a language arts objective, writing clear sequential directions by using these devices. She documented her students' learning by videotaping their actions and comments. She also made copies of their writings and drawings as they designed motions, predicted graphs, and tested their predictions.

An earlier version of this chaper was presented at the 2002 National Association for Research in Science Teaching annual meeting in New Orleans.

Teaching young children is a daily challenge, yet very rewarding. I always strive to find ways to keep my students motivated because I feel that motivation is the driving force that enables students to make good progress, and I want to help all of my students do so, especially those students who struggle academically. When I wrote this account, I was teaching at Hyattsville Elementary School in Prince George's County, Maryland, where my first-grade students came from many different cultures.

I know I must present material in a variety of ways to ensure that I give every learner in my care the opportunity to make progress. This has led me to become involved in a line of practice in teaching coined *teacher research* (Cochran-Smith and Lytle 1993; Mills 2000) in which I focus specifically on my students as individual learners. Along with this, I continuously analyze my practice—trying to make the learning environment optimal for everyone. Data collection enables me to delve more deeply into each child's reactions and responses as I develop or implement activities. My data sources are student work samples, audiotapes, videotapes, photographs, interviews, surveys, anecdotal notes, and journals.

Using Motion Detectors

When I first began doing teacher research, through a seminar sponsored by the University of Maryland, I met a teacher, Deborah Roberts, who was documenting how she was using motion detectors with her students (Roberts 1998 and Chapter 13). A motion detector uses infrared signals to detect where an object is. The detector sends signals to a computer, which displays a line graph representing the motion—position versus time, velocity versus time, or acceleration versus time, or all three. The following school year, I developed ways to use motion detectors with my first-grade students. I felt that this technology would be an excellent tool to help motivate all of my students.

First, I connected the motion detector to a computer, along with a graphing program developed to go with it *(http://elementary.vernier.com)*. Next, I briefly discussed motion detectors in general. Then, I gave a classroom full of excited students permission to move in front of the detector any way they chose to move—with just a few safety reminders. Finally, the students were on their way to conversations about the lines that the computer displayed on the position-versus-time graph as they moved in front of the motion detector. My goals for this activity were twofold: engagement and explanation. I wanted the students' full attention, and I wanted them to talk about what they discovered. I had no intention to discuss x-axes or y-axes, or, for that matter, go into great depth about line graphs. That could come later.

Interpreting Line Graphs

At the onset of their "play," it was apparent that I had discovered something that kept the interest of the entire class. Each student was wholeheartedly engaged in what was going on. Not one student was unhappy or unwilling to participate. Having every student engaged at the same time is a teacher's dream! Initially they discussed the resemblance of their line graphs to things they knew—they noticed "mountains" and "icicles," "a cow's udder," "lots of letter *M*s," "the letter *W*," "those things in caves that hang down." One student even said that the lines "look like stocks." (When I agreed, she added that her father knew about stocks.) They couldn't get enough.

These discussions eventually began to shift. The students began making observations about what one person's line graph looked like compared to another person's graph. We began to test their thinking. How could a person moving in front of the motion detector recreate the same line graph? Could another person make a line graph just like a previous one? Was anyone willing to make a prediction about what a line would look like if someone moved a certain way? These new conversations were actually interpretations of the position-versus-time line graphs. They had to think about their movement in relation to what the lines looked like (Hogan 1999, 2001). They were learning how to interpret line graphs by participating in this activity, as has been reported for other students in other research (Mokros and Tinker 1987).

They began to notice that, when someone moved away from the motion detector, the line "went up." When someone moved toward the motion detector, the line "went down." When someone stood still, the line "went straight." They were working together to gain understanding about these things, and I was impressed. I allowed the conversations to continue as I gave them more opportunities to participate. Students moved to specific directions, first making some predictions as to what the line graph would look like when they were finished.

Integrating Writing

I always try to integrate writing into every subject so I created a written task for this activity. The students were given a paper on which they could draw and write about their experience with the motion detector. I had them write down their predictions, observations, and thoughts as we worked together. I knew that the students had some new understandings of the relationship between the line graph and their own movements, and they demonstrated this as they wrote about their thinking. One student wrote (spelling corrected) "When I went in front of the motion detector, it made a straight line when I stood still. When I went backwards, it made a line that went up. When I went forward, the line went down." (See Figure 1.)

Students who were unable to write complete sentences and often agonized over any writing assignment clearly demonstrated, in writing, without any complaints, that they understood the connection between their movement and the line. One student wrote, "stood still, straight." The written part of this activity not only documented the students' thinking about the relationship between their movements and the line graph, but it helped me stay focused on my goals for the lesson. It also reinforced my thoughts about first graders and writing: Given the right topic all students can enjoy writing and view themselves as writers.

Learning to Write Clear Sequential Directions

With this in mind, I extended this activity by collaborating with a colleague, Pamela Barton, the reading specialist at Hyattsville Elementary School. We wanted to know if using a motion detector would help students learn to write clear sequential directions, a first-grade language arts learning outcome.

Figure 1: Student observation of motion detector

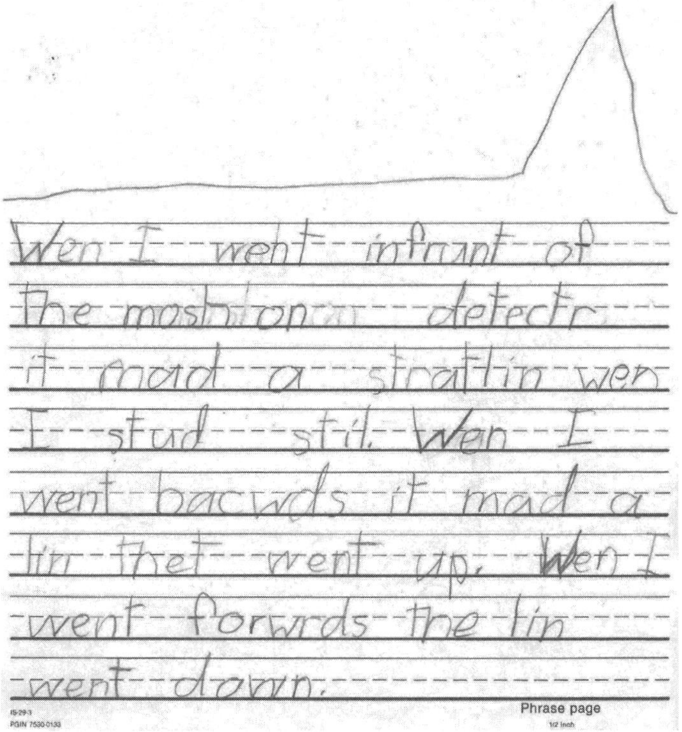

Wen I went infrunt of the moshon detectr it mad a strattin wen I stud stil. Wen I went bacwds it mad a hir thet went up. Wen I went forwrds the tin went down.

First we led an oral exercise. The students practiced giving directions to each other about how to get from one place in the classroom to another place. They could clearly see that they were missing important information about how to do this. Merely saying, "Go over there and turn right" wasn't enough. They needed more specific words.

Next, we had them write directions down, telling someone how to get from one room in the building to another room. They were reminded about trying to add enough information so that the person could easily get from the starting point to the final destination. They were able to test their directions by walking through them, either while writing them or when they were finished. Still, they saw that there was something missing.

From here Pam and I linked the process of writing clear sequential directions back to the motion detector. We gave the students the necessary sequential words (*first, next, then, last*) and guided them as they wrote sequential directions about their movement in front of the motion detector. A student wrote, "First I go backwards. Next I stand still. Then I go forward. Last I stand still." (See Figure 2.)

Figure 2: Student observation of motion detector

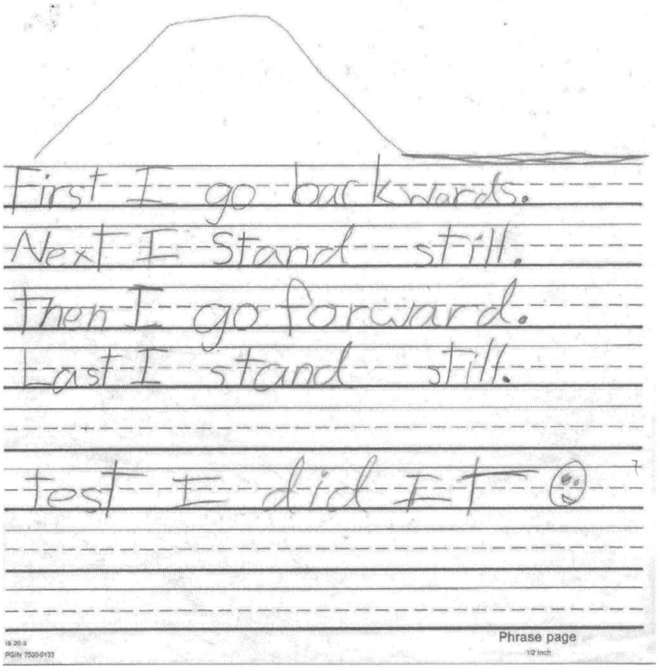

They tested what they had written and were able to see that these words helped them give clear-cut directions.

After this, we had them write directions again, telling someone how to get from one room in the building to another room, using these same sequential words. As with previous activities, all students attempted to write clear directions. Nobody gave up. Some students paired together for support, while others eagerly set out alone to master the task at hand. A student wrote: "First go out the door and go left. Next go past the lunchroom. Then go through the stairs. Then go down the hall. Then go to the first class on the left and stop. Last, look around, you are there, go in." Every student was interested in completing the assignment and able to write better directions than on his or her first attempt. Those children who had trouble actually writing down their words because of their poor writing abilities also were able to give better directions than they had on their first attempts.

Table 1: Standards demonstrated by motion studies

The following National Mathematics Content Standards were demonstrated:
- Attention to data analysis, statistics, and probability.
- Use communication to foster understanding of mathematics.

The following Maryland State Performance Standard for mathematics was demonstrated:
- Interpret, compare and make predictions based on tables and graphs.

The following National English/Language Arts Content Standard was demonstrated:
- Generate written communication and use various stages of the writing process.

The following Maryland State Performance Standards for English/Language Arts was demonstrated:
- Writing: students produce informational writing that demonstrates an awareness of audience, purpose, and form using stages of the writing process as needed.

The following National Science Education Teaching Standards were met. They complement the National Science Education Content Standards for Science as Inquiry:
- Standard A: Teachers of science plan inquiry-based science activities.
- Standard B: Teachers of science guide and facilitate learning science.
- Standard C: Teachers of science engage in ongoing assessment of their teaching and of student learning.
- Standard D: Teachers of science design and manage learning environments that provide students with the time, space, and resources needed for learning science.
- Standard E: Teachers of science develop a community of science learners that reflect the intellectual rigor of scientific inquiry and the attitudes and social values conducive to science learning.
- Standard F: Teachers of science actively participate in the ongoing planning and development of the school science program.

The following Maryland State Performance Standards for Science were met:
- Employ the language, instruments, methods, and materials of science for collecting, organizing, interpreting, and communicating information.
- Demonstrate ways of thinking and acting inherent in the practice of science.

Enacting Standards

When educators consciously work hard for the benefit of all of their students, it is easy to see that national as well as local standards can be met. For these activities, English/language arts, mathematics, and science were integrated (see Table 1). Standards help educators question, think about, and act upon their thoughts about their students' learning.

Indeed, my students were willing to work hard on these assignments. I feel that I would not have had the attention of all of my students if it had not been for the use of the motion detector as a tool for teaching this type of writing activity. Although I might have been able to get the same concept across to many students without this piece of technology, I know that, *because* I used this piece of technology, I was able to get also the full attention of those students who would normally grimace at the mere thought that they had to do some writing. This alone is the reason I strongly advocate that all educators find ways to reach all of their students. With perseverance, it is possible to find ways to help every student make progress. When my students have a feeling of accomplishment, it makes all of the hard work worthwhile.

Recently, at a teacher researcher conference, someone said to me adamantly, "But we don't need these [motion detectors] to help students learn about graphs or to learn to write clear directions." My response to this person was, "No, we don't, but I do." My students needed it too. And that is what we should do as educators—find ways to help our students. Likewise, if we share our experiences, we can help motivate each other to continue finding ways to present material to our students, ensuring every student is given the opportunity to be successful.

Reflections

One element of teacher research is gathering evidence. Kathleen collected student work and then copied it for use in this research project. She paid attention to what her students were saying, and she recorded what they said on audiotape and videotape. She thought about what was happening in her classroom and kept a journal of her thoughts. Each of these evidence-gathering practices is an example of how the process of doing teacher research takes a part of daily teaching practice and develops it in such a way that it can be captured, shared, and revisited after time has passed. Kathleen deepened her teaching practice by her conscious methods of gathering classroom evidence.

As a classroom teacher, Kathleen couldn't focus on just one aspect of her teaching and neglect the others. She was thinking about student engagement, about collaborating with her reading specialist, about teaching graphing and literacy simultaneously, and about the national and state standards she was required to address. She integrated her evidence-gathering practices into all these areas of her teaching practice.

References

Cochran-Smith, M., and S. Lytle. 1993. *Inside/outside: Teacher research and knowledge.* New York: Teachers College Press.

Hogan, K. 1999. Exactly how can an educator use a motion detector as a teaching tool with students? Seminar paper, University of Maryland.

Hogan, K. 2001. Learning in motion. *ENC focus: A Magazine for Classroom Innovators, New*

Horizons in Mathematics And Science education 8(4): 40–42.

Maryland State Department of Education. n.d. *Maryland State Performance Standards*. Retrieved 16 March 2002 from *www.msde.state.md.us*.

Mills, G. 2000. *Action research: A guide for the teacher researcher*. Englewood Cliffs, NJ: Prentice-Hall.

Mokros, J.R., and R.F. Tinker. 1987. The impact of microcomputer-based labs on children's ability to interpret graphs. *Journal of Research on Science Teaching* 24: 369–383.

National Council for Teachers of English (NCTE). 2001. *The standards for the English languages arts*. Retrieved March 16, 2002, from *www.ncte.org*.

National Council of Teachers of Mathematics (NCTM). 2001. *Principles and standards for teachers of mathematics*. Retrieved March 16, 2002, from *www.nctm.org*.

National Research Council (NRC). 1996. *National Science Education Standards*. Washington, DC: National Academy Press. Retrieved July 18, 2006, from *www.nap.edu/html/nses*.

Roberts, D. 1998. Physics and first graders—what a good match! Paper presented at annual meeting of American Educational Research Association, San Diego.

Chapter 2

Reading, Writing, Comprehension, and Confidence
—Achieved in Science Contexts

Elizabeth Kline

When Elizabeth Kline wrote this, she was a fifth-grade teacher in Prince George's County, Maryland. A desire to integrate scientific concepts in a curriculum dominated by reading, writing, and mathematics motivated her to change the way she taught a mandated unit on the Moon. She invited her students to make a book. She documented their learning, continually assessing student understanding in the process. The excitement in the class was palpable as students used their creativity while they integrated science and literacy. The next year, when the unit began, her new students often consulted the book and enjoyed reading other fifth graders' interpretation of the subject matter. In this chapter, Elizabeth describes the process by which she engaged her students in literacy learning in a science context.

What can a teacher do in a classroom of average readers and writers who are tackling difficult scientific concepts to build their confidence as readers, writers, and scientists? Write a science textbook of course.

We were working through a unit on the Moon from my county's mandated science curriculum. The students did an investigation in which one student used a Styrofoam ball attached to a pencil to represent the Moon and another student held a flashlight to represent the Sun. The student holding the ball moon moved the ball to predetermined angles and made a drawing of the lit portion of the ball that the student saw at each stop. In the end the students saw that the ball moon went through phases. We also spent a month recording the Moon's appearance in the sky and compared that with what we saw with the ball moon in class. Many children also brought in Moon charts from the internet.

I wanted to make the reading material in this unit more accessible and real to my students, most of whom came from low-income and full-time working families. Essentially my plan was to write a book for the next year's fifth-grade class in which my students would have the chance to explain in their own vernacular what they learned and to add literacy elements to the book they would like to have had in their own resources—essentially make the ultimate resource for the next year's class. This was also a way for me to explore some of the issues my colleagues and I had been discussing in a master's course about integrating science and literacy learning (Saul 2004; Thier and Daviss 2002; Wellington and Osborne 2001).

Identifying Useful Text Elements

To begin this project, I gave my students everything I could find that had to do with science: trade books, textbooks, "eyewitness" books, and science magazines. I then asked them to look over these examples of science writing and note what they liked about each. I prepared to record their responses on one sheet of chart paper, but, as I began to listen and record their observations, I was astounded. We filled the whole board with elements they felt were important and that they thought other fifth graders would want to see. They hit the basics: title, subtitles, pictures, captions, and diagrams. What I was so excited to hear were the extras they thought we should include: amazing facts and investigations that kids could do at home. My "average" readers and writers wanted to make sure we used vocabulary that other fifth graders could understand, stayed on topic, and used examples as much as possible. After creating this huge list, I was convinced I was doing the right thing. Plus my students' excitement to begin working was high!

Getting Started Writing a Book

We got started right away. The students worked first on the introductory vocabulary that the county's science curriculum called for them to learn. *Rotation, revolution, orbit, ellipse, satellite,* and *axis* were the words. They were off to explain these terms in their own way and to show how the ideas could be understood. What I saw was great. The students were excited and involved with writing about the concepts with which we had been working. As the first work session came to a close, I felt secure with what they had accomplished.

The next day, I gave my authors a deadline of that afternoon to complete rough drafts of their pages. I explained that they would be trading work and peer editing. As I made my way throughout the classroom, I saw the products were varied: Illustrations and design were strong in some, while extra scientific research was evident in others. One constant was that everyone had put time into creating projects the readers could do at home to further their understanding. This showed they had comprehended the information enough to apply it to practical use. To explain *orbit*, for example, a group of students suggested getting a ball, making a circle with a few friends, putting one person in the middle, and passing the ball around the circle. The ball traveling around the person standing would be making an orbit around that person.

Peer Editing

I was eager to have my students see what their classmates had done, in hopes it would spark the desire to make some work look better or to improve the information presented. I placed each group's work on a clipboard and passed the clipboards to different groups. An editing sheet asked students to look at the pages as next year's fifth graders would. They were to tell what they might think of the pages just by looking, what they liked about them, and what they didn't like. Student comments included suggestions on ways to improve the information presented, advice to remember who the audience would be, indications of captions needed, reminders of grammar, and accolades for pictures, amazing facts, and at-home investigations.

Students returned their evaluations, and the authors used them to make improvements for their final drafts. The drafts showed that many had used their classmates' suggestions for revising diagrams or adding illustrations. When the book was complete, I asked my students to complete a survey about this first writing experience. This survey assessed their feelings about science comprehension, writing, and ways they found their information. Most students said they enjoyed creating chapters for the book. They felt they got to show what they knew through the book and that, while they were working, they felt like good writers. About half the class commented that they found out something new while working: "I learned that the Moon has little robot machines coming to it to take pictures," and "When I do this chapter in my head, I don't really know, and when I write it on paper it seems like I know everything."

Inviting Colleagues' Interpretations

When I discussed the students' first drafts with colleagues in our science and literacy seminar, they pointed out to me what a great resource these were for gauging students' understanding. Upon further viewing, we recognized that there was a misconception about how the planets orbit the Sun. One group's illustration showed all the planets lined up in one orbital path around the Sun. So before beginning the next chapter of writing, I had that group of students create their illustration on the board for the whole class to see. Then we looked at the idea they were trying to communicate and figured out what was wrong with that idea and how to fix it. In this moment, I was able to help my students with a misconception that would not have been evident without this work that we were completing.

Increasing the Challenge and Complexity

When beginning the next book, I wanted to give the students a bit more freedom in creating. They were able to choose their work partners as well as the topic about which they would be writing. We focused on the three main topics we had worked on: why the Moon shines, what the Moon's phases are, and what the properties of the Moon's surface are. As part of this unit, the students had become acquainted with two new trade books, and I was excited to see them reach out to these additional resources when we began our work on the book. They also were more willing to access the internet for information and located some beneficial websites. One site would display Moon phase calendars for any month of the year and for any year. Even as the concepts became more challenging, their excitement remained high. One student said, "Something I did like about writing the pages was that we got to do our own thing for once instead of working in a boring science booklet."

Because the concepts had become a bit more complex, I became more involved. Before the students began drafting their pages, I asked them to show me their facts so we could check for accuracy. Students were using the thesaurus to create catchy titles for their pages. As vocabulary became more challenging for some, conversations became intense with students learning from one another. In one conversation I overheard, a student reminded his classmates that we couldn't just say *invisible*, but that we needed to explain what this meant to the readers so they would better understand.

The editing process was a bit more difficult this time around. I found myself encouraging the children to be honest and give criticism so that their peers could improve their work. Their critiques became very specific, pointing out misconceptions in illustrations or difficult-to-understand passages. Many became seekers of missing text features, which can help a reader, such as subtitles and bold letters. I am pleased to report that, in the end, the second part of the book matched the first and the pages were well done, well thought out, and showed great comprehension of the science concepts.

I surveyed and interviewed my students to assess the benefits of the project. The survey showed that most students felt like good writers while they were working on the pages and that they felt they were able to show everything they knew. Remarkably enough, 27 of the 30 I interviewed felt they understood what they had written about. One said, "I enjoyed working with my partners because they helped me with some things that I did not know before." While looking for information for their pages, students also had reached out to find new information, using the internet, using materials they found in the library, and interviewing staff.

Reflecting on the Book-Making Process

As we wrapped up the project, I collected and reflected on what we had accomplished and I was pleased with our outcome. When I began this project, I was concerned with the students getting a chance to work further with the science concepts and to use text features in their writing. I was not expecting excitement about the subject matter and the confidence my student writers gained. One of my writers said, "I enjoyed writing the pages because it improved my story-writing skills and helped me get ideas for my next *Megaman* stories #3."

The old adage says "The proof is in the pudding," and our project proved this beyond my expectations. About a week after putting the book together, we were working on a cumulative assessment task about the science concepts we had covered. I was excited to see the students go to the class book as a resource to help them complete their work. The book was indeed immediately a fruitful resource, although I hadn't expected it to be used until the next year.

From this experience, I would say using writing in a science context gave the children a chance to write in a less formal setting than a typical writing lesson. Working with classmates or by themselves and creating work that is meaningful helped to create a sense of excitement and importance. One of the best results was the learning, from one another and individually, that took place. As one student said, "I enjoyed this project because other people will have an easier time figuring out this stuff."

Reflections

One element of teacher research is sharing findings with colleagues. When Elizabeth brought the students' first drafts to share with colleagues in her master's program, the group discussion helped her interpret the data she was collecting, and she used the ideas from the group to inform her teaching. She eventually wrote up her study in the paper that became this chapter, but she didn't need a final version of her findings to share what she was seeing. The sharing of student work, informally with another teacher, or more formally in meetings at the school, is a teacher practice that is a part of teacher research. If carried into a more formal version, this element can become a presentation at a conference or a paper written for publication (see Table 1 in the Preface).

Teachers are often faced with mandates that they believe are not good teaching practices. However, they are required to implement the mandates by their district or state. In Elizabeth's narrative, the mandated curriculum required an introduction of scientific vocabulary that was not part of her students' repertoire. Her creative way of meeting this requirement enacted a child-centered approach that addressed student engagement and confidence while integrating science and literacy learning.

References

Saul, W., ed. 2004. *Crossing borders in literacy and science instruction*. Newark, DE: International Reading Association; Arlington, VA: NSTA Press.

Thier, M., and B. Daviss. 2002. *The new science literacy: Using language skills to help students learn science*. Portsmouth, NH: Heinemann.

Wellington, J., and J. Osborne. 2001. *Language and literacy in science education*. Philadelphia: Open University Press.

Chapter 3

Fourth-Grade Scientists Investigate Electric Circuits

Trisha Kagey Boswell

Trisha Kagey Boswell is a third-grade teacher at an elementary school in Montgomery County, Maryland, where she has taught for eight years. Her school is an art-integrated magnet school. When she wrote this chapter, she was a first-year teacher, teaching fourth grade. She reflects on trying to create in her own classroom the inquiry experiences she enjoyed in a physics course as a part of her preservice program. She also describes her efforts at tracking the influence of such inquiry-based instruction by documenting changes in her students' understandings of what scientists do. Writing in the middle of a unit on electric circuits, she comments upon what they had done so far, describes what they were in the process of doing, and anticipates an event in which the students would be communicating their findings.

Abstract

As a first-year teacher, I am curious about how I can model an authentic scientific inquiry experience with my fourth-grade students. We began our exploration of electric circuits with questions that the students asked. Cooperative groups are developing hypotheses and designing investigations to answer their questions. Students will communicate their results at a "Scientists' Conference." In this case study, I am monitoring how students perceive themselves as scientists as they figure things out. Data sources include the student displays, their reflections in their journals, and taped discussions.

Generating Student Questions

One day as my fourth graders were finishing an assessment from a previous unit, I asked them to generate questions they had about electricity for a bulletin board titled "What We Want to Know About Electricity." I was preoccupied with the students' finishing the assessment and was not monitoring the increasingly large group of children who were busy writing and illustrating their questions on construction paper. Then David walked up to me with an eager smile, "I have a question, Ms. Kagey. How can you get electricity in an airplane?" I followed his thought process. Electricity comes from the ground, electrical plugs, and power lines. How can electricity reach an airplane? I smiled like a teacher who lets her children plan her lessons.

I am fascinated by students' scientific questions. They reveal so much about a student's understanding, misconceptions, and curiosity. I decided to plan an electricity unit that focused on investigating our questions about electricity. Marletta Iwasyk examined the role of student questions to direct their own learning. "Questioning techniques can be used by students to learn how to ask questions of themselves or of others to investigate or explore a topic of interest" (Iwasyk 1997, p. 46). My goal was connected to the National Science Education Standards Teaching Standard E: "Teachers of science develop communities of science learners that reflect the intellectual rigor of scientific inquiry and the attitudes and social values conducive to science learning" (NRC 1996, p. 45). Teaching Standard E recognizes the influence of community in the learning of science as well as the importance of developing students' attitudes toward science.

As we began our unit, my students wrote questions in KWH charts (what I *know*, what I *want* to know, and *how* I am going to find out). We also wrote in our science journals during and at the conclusion of our experiments. Lastly, I asked my students to choose 10 questions that they were interested in investigating connected with electric circuits. From those, they chose one question to investigate and to communicate their results in a Scientists' Conference that would be a crucial conclusion to our investigation. I was very interested in watching my students' progress through the stages of scientific inquiry. I was curious about my role as their teacher in advocating for their confidence in science.

Inquiring in My College Physics Class

While I was attending college, I participated in two classes that shaped the way I want to teach science to my elementary school students. My colleagues enthusiastically recommended a science elective titled "Physics for Elementary School Teachers." I had taken physics in high school and found the class confusing and frustrating. Because of this experience, I was hesitant to take a physics class. But the college class was taught differently than any other science class that I have taken. We designed our own experiments and created our own formulas. The constants in the formulas were values that were results of experiments we did in class. We also formulated our own definitions for scientific terms. (This can be harder than it sounds.) It was common knowledge that the professor and teaching assistants were not the sources of answers. If we asked a question, they would answer it with a question. If an experiment was necessary to answer the question, they would point us to the materials. It was because we were able to design our own experiments and to find results using equations we created that the class equipped us with a confidence in science that I had never before known.

Teacher Research

Reflecting in My Science Teaching Methods Course

My science-teaching methods course revealed to me the methods of scientific inquiry, and I quickly made the connection to my physics course. In my methods course, I designed projects that modeled the methods of scientific inquiry and the National Science Education Standards. I reflected upon my own successful learning experiences and developed my own recommendations for science teaching. I felt I was prepared to teach science to my new fourth graders. I was not aware of the complexity of translating my recommendations for science teaching as well as the National Science Education Standards into a unit on electric circuits.

Documenting My Students' Perceptions of Scientists

I found the unit on electric circuits to be a fascinating one for scientific inquiry. My fourth graders had continual experiences with electricity but almost no idea how it worked. I think 10-year-olds see electricity as similar to the telephone and the internet. They accept it as a magical unknown or a subject for scientists. I was motivated to give my students the confidence in science that my physics class had given me. I wanted to measure my students' perceptions of scientists and see how I could get them to identify themselves as scientists. I also needed to establish my role as their science teacher. I was not there to answer their questions nor was I there to watch passively. I needed to negotiate a role as an instigator, a facilitator, a questioner, and an audience to whom they could communicate their scientific ideas.

I wanted to document my students' attitudes about the roles of scientists and the qualities that make a scientist. I asked them to respond to the question, "What is a scientist?" I found many commonalities in their replies. (See Figure 1.) They believed that scientists are experimenting and researching to serve the world: "Scientists help the world to understand more about the world." What interested me most was that my students saw scientists as adult professionals who work in a laboratory. If asked, I believed they would not identify themselves as scientists. I was eager to ask them the same question after our Scientists' Conference to see how their definitions differed.

Figure 1: Example student responses to "What is a scientist?" (spelling uncorrected

"A scientist is someone who uses science to do their job. A scientist may use science to develop medicines or study plant life or animals. Scientist develop facts that the world uses to do good. Scientists are working on a cure for cancer right now. Scientists may study animals for a while and then they may try to make a medicine or write a report to help animals. Scientist help the world to understand more about the world."

"I think a scientist is a persin who does exsperaments and discovers new things in the world. He is also a persen who works lab and offices."

"A scientist is someone who is smart, makes good observations and is scientific. A scientist also has graduated from college. A scientist finds out information by using items, such as chemicals. Sometimes they find new objects and it may cure things. Scientists are help. They sometimes dig to find something. No matter what, scientists observe things and find out data. There are many different kinds of scientists such as marine biologists. Most of the time scientists study nature. Some scientists study plants or water."

Documenting Student Questions About Electric Circuits

To record my students' questions and insights, I quickly established science journals. My students had continually evolving notebooks that contained all of their experiments, data, evidence, questions, ideas, and reflections. It was important that they could revisit their previous entries for reflection. My students needed some background knowledge with the electric circuits; therefore we did a couple of experiments with batteries and bulbs. Periodically, I would ask them to write down questions they had about electric circuits. I noticed that many of the factual questions such as "Who invented electricity?" began to fade and gradually more complicated questions followed. Their questions would further our experiments and reflect their broadening understanding. After we did an experiment lighting a small lightbulb with a battery and wire, they asked, "How many batteries would it take to light a regular lightbulb? What if you hooked up two batteries? What is inside a battery?" They had a new range of materials to be curious about. The battery holders and Fahenstock clips became prevalent in their questions.

I challenged my students to think of 10 questions that they wanted to ask about electric circuits. (See Figures 2 and 3.) They revisited their entries in their science journals and looked at the KWH charts around the room. I wandered the room, reading their lists and marveling at their intellectual curiosity. I asked them to form cooperative groups and share their questions. The groups were then expected to choose one question they wished to investigate. I wanted to define the parameters for a good research question, without limiting them or decreasing their confidence in science. I instructed them to choose a question that they could answer with an in-class investigation. They were very motivated, and my budding scientists began to deliberate diligently.

Figure 2: A student's list of questions

1. What is the biggest circuit?
2. Will our 8 battery experiment work with 2 bulbs?
3. Does the circuit size affect the lightbulb?
4. Can you use 4 bulbs and 2 rows of batteries?
5. Does the type of battery matter?
6. Are there certain types of wires needed?
7. How long will one small bulb stay lit with 1 battery?
8. How do flashlights work?
9. Will extra strength batteries work best?
10. Can a battery and a wire work elsewhere?
11. Can you make your own flashlight?
    * I think so!*
12. What does electrical tape do?

Figure 3: Another student's list of questions

1. What is solar power? How does it get power by the sun?
2. How do you get power out of a potato?
3. Are alarms electricity?
4. Do wires and batteries carry power?
5. What do batteries have inside them?
6. Why do full circuits only work?
7. Does gas relate to electricity?
8. Can electricity run out?
9. Can you break electricity?
10. Does electricity hurt you?

As my children discussed, it was sometimes necessary for me to help them to reorganize their questions. I also found a couple of students with questions to which they already knew the answers. I didn't review all of their questions until after we designed our experiments. I took their science journals home for Sunday reading. From their lists of 10 questions, I found inquiries that fell into three categories. Some students' curiosity led them to questions that they could not answer in the elementary school experimentation setting. They wanted to know

- What is inside of a battery?
- Does gas relate to electricity?
- How fast does electricity travel?
- Why can we see lightning and lightbulbs and not electricity?
- Can electricity run out? How does a telephone, a clock, solar power, a VCR work?

These are questions that can be answered through research in books, with professionals, and with the internet, but I wanted to eliminate questions like these from this immediate project to focus on questions that could be answered through experimentation. They also asked questions that I believed to be either part of their prior knowledge or answerable with minor research. Many of these simple research questions began, "Who invented...." I also found questions that should be in their current understanding either through life experience or class experiments. Some examples were

- What kinds of toys have electricity?
- How many ways can you make light with a battery, wire, and lightbulb?
- How do you form a circuit?
- Can electricity hurt you?

I found many questions that were appropriate for fourth-grade study because they could be investigated in class safely with easy-to-find materials and they made connections to the electric circuits curriculum that I was supposed to be teaching. They asked

- Why does a lightbulb sometimes blow up?
- Why do only "full circuits" work?
- How does a flashlight work?
- Can an AA battery work the same as a D battery to light a lightbulb?
- How does a switch turn on a lightbulb?

Also present in the majority of my students' list of questions was connecting electricity to the potato. They had heard a rumor that it is possible to light a lightbulb with citrus fruits or a potato. Many students wanted to know if or how this could work. Also included in this category were the students who wanted to apply what they knew about batteries to create a product such as an alarm, a doorbell, a flashlight, or a game. I was initially apprehensive when my students came up with these questions. I wondered if they were trying to compete with each other or wanting to buy "science kits" from a toy store to create their electric machines.

Experimenting

On experimentation day my apprehension ceased. Was it my role to decide my students' questions? If I wanted them to generate their own questions for experimentation, it required some trust on my part that they were motivated by curiosity. There were variables that I could not regulate. Students were enthusiastic and shared their enthusiasm with friends and family. These unofficial group members contributed to my students' experiments. My students were still learning much about electric circuits through scientific inquiry. I felt that their scientific confidence needed to originate from their exploring their own questions as mine had in physics class. It was not that simple. Two students began creating their "game" on the weekend. They bought a science kit and followed the directions to wire it. From this experience, they learned about insulators, conductors, wiring, and the effects of different batteries, and they couldn't wait to share their discoveries with their class. They felt intense pride in and a sense of accomplishment from their success. Meanwhile, one group connected a whole bag of potatoes to a lightbulb without getting the bulb to light. They were able to identify when they were making errors in their connections, but their question, "How can you light a lightbulb with a potato?" remained unanswered.

Planning for a Scientists' Conference

My students were to present their question, hypothesis, data, summary, and new questions on a poster board to serve as a reference for discussion at our Scientists' Conference. I anticipated rich conversations among my young scientists as they shared their investigations.

Reflections

Questioning is an element of teacher research. Trisha describes her own questions about her practice: How can she model authentic scientific inquiry with her students? How do students perceive themselves as scientists as they try to figure things out? How can she use student questions to guide a unit about a particular science concept? The question about student questions reveals a curiosity not only about her own practice, but also about the nature of inquiry and its role in student learning. A teacher who is conducting an inquiry about her students' conducting an inquiry is a model of learning for her students. Trisha is putting into her own practice the inquiry into inquiry that her college physics teacher had modeled as he engaged prospective teachers in learning science through inquiry.

Teaching science through inquiry presents challenges even to the most experienced of teachers. In the section "Experimenting," Trisha considers some of the challenges that occurred when she actually had students ask questions and investigate their own questions. She had to figure out how to incorporate unanticipated contributions, she wanted to encourage them without quashing their pride, and she showed what happens when she opened up her practice to this kind of ongoing inquiry.

References

Iwasyk, M. 1997. Kids questioning kids: "Experts" sharing. *Science and Children*, 35(1): 42–46.

National Research Council (NRC). 1996. *National Science Education Standards*. Washington, DC: National Academy Press.

National Science Resources Center (NSRC). 1991. *Electric circuits*. Washington, DC: NSRC.

Chapter 4

Understanding Condensation

Monica Hartman

Monica Hartman, Assistant Director for Science in St. Clair County, Michigan, conducted this research while she was the learning specialist in a small suburban district just outside a large midwestern city. While teaching full time in this district she was also completing her doctoral program in education at the University of Michigan. In this chapter, she tells the story of a "science talk" about condensation among fifth graders. She acted as a source and facilitator of change as she and the fifth-grade teacher worked collaboratively to help students share responsibility for their own learning. She describes their continual assessment of student understanding that occurred as their students struggled to explain observations and as they, the teachers, carefully resisted the temptation to end the struggle by saying "that's right!"

As the learning specialist in my district, I helped teachers develop their science teaching practices and modeled standards-based science lessons for elementary and middle school teachers. The *National Science Education Standards* (NRC 1996) describe what teachers of science at all grade levels should know and be able to do. They include six areas:

- The planning of inquiry-based science programs
- The actions taken to guide and facilitate student learning
- The assessments made of teaching and student learning
- The development of environments that enable students to learn science
- The creation of communities of science learners
- The planning and development of the school science program (NRC 1996, p. 4)

These formed the framework for my professional development efforts.

Research describes many benefits of collaboration. A collaborative learning environment can create multiple zones of proximal development (Vygotsky 1978) so students can learn from one another as well as the teacher, unlike in traditional classrooms in which students compete against each other. Within collaborative groups, disagreements over ideas, answers, and ways to solve a problem are likely to arise. This is desirable because conceptual change is more likely to occur in environments that encourage questioning, evaluating, criticizing, and in which dissatisfaction with the existing state of knowledge exists (Brown and Palincsar 1989). Another benefit of collaboration is that the cognitive load is spread among the members, enabling a higher level of achievement than would otherwise be possible (Wood et al. 1976).

The lesson described further on was a science talk, an idea developed by Karen Gallas (1995). Gallas found that "the kinds of talk and thinking that children engage in when studying science naturally parallel what both practicing scientists and historians of science report" (p. 13). Science is a process of developing and evaluating theories, and science facts are socially constructed through the process of confrontation and negotiation (Latour and Woolgar 1986). Because the teacher does not evaluate students' statements during the science talk, more students have an opportunity to share their ideas. Discourse during the science talk makes student thinking visible (Collins, Brown, and Holum 1991). They listen to competing theories suggested by their classmates. Even when these competing theories are wrong, students benefit by contrasting them to the scientific theory. Duckworth (1996) argues that

> Exploring ideas can only be to the good, even if it takes time. Wrong ideas, moreover, can only be productive. Any wrong idea that is corrected provides far more depth than if one never had a wrong idea to begin with. (p. 71)

Science talks can create a community of learners, provide an environment that enables student inquiry and learning, and give teachers opportunities for formative assessment. For this study, I examined two issues: How does students' understanding of condensation develop during a science talk? and How can I better facilitate a science talk to help students develop deeper understanding?

Context of the Investigation

I modeled this science talk for a first-year teacher. This was the first science talk for the students and for me. Nineteen students were present—15 Caucasian, 3 Hispanic, and 1 Arabic. Forty percent of the students in this district received reduced-price or free lunches. These fifth graders were studying phase changes and would soon be introduced to the water cycle. Students at this age find it difficult to understand that there is water vapor in the air and that this water vapor can condense on cold objects. They often believe that the water that forms on the outside of their cold drink cup comes from the melting ice inside it. Expecting this idea from the students, I planned a *pivotal case* (Linn and Hsi 2000). A pivotal case is an example that teachers can use to pivot or shift students' thinking from a less-productive idea to a more-productive one. In this case, because I predicted that students would say that water forming on the outside of a container would come from the melted ice inside it, I filled the container with water colored blue and then froze it. During the discussion, students had the opportunity to hold this container and directly observe the phenomena of condensation. If the students responded that the water on the outside of the container came from the melted ice inside, I could ask them why the water was not blue.

The classroom teacher videotaped the science talk and the activity afterwards. This activity involved small groups of students building a model of the water cycle using containers of blue ice similar to the one used in the talk. The science talk was transcribed and analyzed for the development of students' ideas about condensation.

Interpreting the Data

The question I—I've referred to myself as "Teacher" in these exchanges—asked the students was:

Teacher: Where does the water on the outside of the container come from?

The first student used the phrase "the water's coming out " and described the melting of the ice within the container as the water source, seeming to hypothesize as expected that the water came through the cup from the ice that had melted inside it:

Omar: I think the water's coming from, OK, the water's coming out 'cause the thing is frozen and it's hot up here. The outside is kind of frozen a little bit. You know how ice melts so the outside? It kind of melts a little bit. So that's why the water's coming out.

Another student offered a different idea that introduced the role of the air from the outside:

Andrea: I think because, OK, because it's wet. There's ice inside and it's cold and the air from the outside gets on it and it gets it wet.

Andrea already seemed to be headed in the right direction. I wondered if the other students would hear her idea and agree. I worried that the science talk would soon end. In the past I probably would have elaborated on her ideas and given the students a more detailed explanation, but I wanted to hear other students' ideas. The goal of a science talk is to let students construct their own knowledge. I knew I should remain quiet. While I was thinking about what I should do, another student questioned her meaning:

Student: You think it's from the heat?
Andrea: Yeah.

Joshua offered an explanation that built on Omar's thinking:

Joshua: The heat would make the ice sort of melt, sort of to make water come out. The ice melts to make water.

The students continued sharing ideas, and it looked like I did not have to worry that the science talk was over. At this point, I asked for clarification:

Teacher: Where's the water coming out of?
Joshua: It's coming from the ice, because the heat is melting the ice.
Teacher: So you're saying the water is coming from the ice that's inside the container?
Joshua: Yes.

Christie proposed that it might have something to do with pressure, but she could not define pressure or explain how that might work. Her idea about pressure led Matthew to hypothesize that the water might have come out by pressing on the lid of the container:

Matthew: I think it comes from out of the seal. When you put the lid back on. And then where it comes from is, it's inside the container so then when you put pressure on top of it, it will start like deforming, I think the word is, and then it just goes over to most of the sides when you press in the middle and so, then the water like … [puts hands on face].

To make it sound more scientific, he made up a word for this—*deforming*. He was not totally convinced about this coinage, as evidenced by his putting his hands over his face and not finishing his last sentence.

Joshua agreed with the pressure idea, but wanted to make sure that heat was included in the new hypothesis:

Joshua: Matthew, I sort of agree with the pressure, but it's sort of the heat that's making it, because the heat hits the container, it makes it get warmer and makes the ice melt.

*Teacher*Research

Most people were happy with the ideas that heat made the ice melt and the water escaped to the outside of the cup:

Laura: I think it's because it's outside. Like it's not in the freezer anymore and it's getting hot and the ice melts and makes water.
Teacher: So when the ice that's inside the container melts, are you saying that the ice turns to water and comes out of the container and gets on the outside?

Laura, Tina, and Kayla nodded yes.

At this point, Christie asked if water was outside the cup before I put it in the freezer. Not knowing what she was trying to figure out, I gave her a lengthy description of the process of filling the container with blue water and freezing it. She then claimed that the water could not come from the inside because it could not come out and therefore it must come from the outside:

Christie: The water doesn't come from the inside.
Teacher: Why not?
Christie: Because it can't come out.
Teacher: If it can't come out from the inside, where is it coming from?
Christie: It's coming from the outside.
Teacher: What's outside?
Christie: I don't know. It's ... kind of with the heat

She still did not know how, but thought it might have something to do with heat and pressure.

Omar was sitting next to Christie, and, while she was talking, he was noticing that when he wiped the bottom of the container, the water came back every time.

Omar: I tried something right now. I wiped the water on the bottom, and then it comes back every time!
Teacher: So why is that happening? The same thing happened to me.
Omar: Because of the ice. It's on the bottom. When the heat hits it, it melts.

This reminded Andrea of a time earlier in the year when her water bottle on her desk was making everything wet. I was in her classroom that day and, knowing that the class would later be studying this phenomenon and because she thought her bottle was leaking, I gave her a scientific explanation of why the water was forming on her bottle. I was impressed that during this science talk she recalled that event and was coming close to describing that it had something to do with the air:

Andrea: I think that when it comes out of the freezer, it's like the frost, not like frost, but the moisture gets on it. Because I had a water bottle that I thought was leaking at school because it was in the freezer all night and I thought it was cracked. But Mrs. Hartman told me it could have been from being in the freezer so long it got wet. Moisture on the outside and the air would make it more water. I think that's what happened with the ice.

I thought she did a better job explaining this at the beginning of the science talk [*Andrea:* I think because, OK, because it's wet. There's ice inside and it's cold and the air from the outside gets on it and it gets it wet.] but I noticed that when I did not respond to her first conjecture early in the talk by saying "that's right," she seemed to think she needed to change it. This may have made the struggle to describe her ideas more difficult. She often would contradict herself and try to include two different ideas in the same sentence. I wondered if the science talk was helping Andrea or confusing her.

Larry offered a new hypothesis about water vapor and said, "The water comes out of it and gets on the outside." He was not sure of himself and offered this conjecture in a quiet voice and banged his hands on the table. Larry did not have a high level of self-esteem. I misunderstood what he said. I thought he was saying that water was coming out of the bottle, but, after listening to the tapes, I'm wondering if he might have had a more scientific understanding and meant to say that water was coming out of the air. I could have probed more about his idea about water vapor.

At this point, I asked why the water on the outside was not blue. Omar was now reminded of the water he had seen on windows that he could write on:

Omar: It does like what it does like on winter days on the window, where it comes from the inside and you can write on it or like on the bus.

Kate offered the idea that the water might be sweat from the outside. When I asked her to explain more, she said "Water comes from …" and then hesitated. Andrea finished Kate's sentence with "moisture in the air."

Andrea seemed to be more convinced of the idea she expressed at the beginning of the talk, and she now got support for this idea from several students who agreed with her. However Omar did not agree and insisted the water was coming from the ice. Ron agreed with Kate's sweat hypothesis:

Ron: When the container, when it's in the freezer, not only the ice gets cold, but the container also gets cold and now the container comes out of the freezer. The container is so cold to where it's so hot that it makes like sweat or water.

Joshua: I sort of agree with Ron, but when ice hits the container, it makes it so cool that the container gets water on it, but it's not blue because the ice is hitting it. The blue water won't come from the inside and come out.

Teacher: So where does the water come from?

Joshua: The water comes from the moisture in the air when the ice is hitting the plastic.

Joshua was thinking out loud and seemed to be in agreement with Andrea. When pushed to explain his thinking, he suggested the water was coming from the moisture in the air.

It appeared that the class was making some progress. More students were now considering the idea that the water came from moisture in the air. Most seemed fairly comfortable sharing their ideas. Then Matthew surprised me with a new idea. Not ready to accept the scientific idea, he suggested the water was coming from the ice in the cooler I brought to school. He thought that the other ice inside the cooler was melting and making the containers wet:

Matthew: I think the water comes from the freezer. The water on the cup comes from the freezer. There's probably ice in the cooler [indicating the cooler I brought from home]. When the ice inside the cooler melts, it kind of gets all wet on the package or container or whatever and that's why it's not blue.

I was more surprised that several other students agreed with Matthew. I began to realize that there were still several students who could not conceptualize this idea of water vapor in the air. Jim then made the suggestion that the water was coming from people's hands.

Melissa, who was very quiet during the talk, took a long time to respond but finally shared her ideas. She described the condensation you see when you open the freezer door as evaporation:

Melissa: Ice has been out so long it started to melt … [very long pause]. Water is coming out and it's starting to melt and evaporate.

Teacher: What do you know about evaporate?

Melissa: Air comes out. Like when you open up the freezer. You see some air come out and that's evaporation.

Jenny: I think when water is coming from out of the air because when you take it out of the freezer, you get hot air from the house and stuff, and that's where it is from.

Other children called it visible air. The science talk seemed to be helping the students connect this phenomenon to their previous experiences. Joshua described how water was forming on his own water bottle and compared it to what happens to the car window in winter and sometimes in summer, depending on the temperature:

Joshua: I was looking at my water bottle [students are allowed to keep drinking water bottles on their desk] and it has the same thing like the blue ice that Larry was talking about. I'm feeling it and looking around. Then I realize that when the heat hits the ice water, it makes something. It might make something like that you get on the car all the time. Like when the heat and the cold mix, it hits the window and it makes the heat from the car hits the car window from the inside and the cold hits the car window from the outside.

Teacher: Would it happen in the summer?
Joshua: It might, it would depend on the temperature.

At this point, I decided to conclude the science talk. Next I made a model of the water cycle with ice from the science talk. During this activity, I gave the scientific explanation for the condensation phenomena, relating it to the ideas expressed during the science talk, but I knew some of the children were still not ready to accept the scientific explanation and would require more instruction with this concept.

Implications for Instruction

My teacher colleague and I were amazed at the process by which many of the children came to realize that the water on the container came from moisture in the air rather than from the melted ice inside it. Many figured this out by questioning, explaining, and listening to one another's ideas. We could see how their ideas about condensation developed, or didn't develop, during the process. We began to question the depth of students' understanding if we as teachers just tell them or if they read about concepts from the textbook.

While transcribing the children's responses, I found there were many ideas that I missed during the talk. By reflecting on those ideas that I heard as well as the ideas that I missed, I am thinking about ways that I could improve my facilitation of science talks.

Not all students developed the scientific explanation at the end of the science talk, but science is a process of developing and evaluating theories. As a teacher, I want to help my students develop scientific ideas and learn to evaluate the ideas of others.

Since this first talk, I have listened to many students share their ideas about condensation. Hearing their ideas has enabled me to look at the concept of condensation through their eyes. I now think about other experiences that could help them develop this concept throughout the curriculum. The variety of explanations expressed by the students during the talk naturally leads to inquiry activities that can be done in the classroom.

Teacher Research

Chapter 4

At the beginning of the science talk most fourth- and fifth-grade students explain that the water forming on the outside of the container comes through the plastic. They know that is has something to do with the heat and the cold, but students need to know that there is water in the air to come to a scientific explanation of condensation. Condensation involves a phase change. As water vapor molecules release their heat energy and cool, they change from a gas to a liquid. This is difficult for young students to understand, because water vapor is invisible and they have not yet learned about molecules.

Younger students observe and study phase changes. They know from experience that, when you warm ice, the solid form of water changes to a liquid form. If the water is heated more, you no longer see it. They may have observed the results of evaporation as water seems to disappear on the blackboard, in puddles, or in the fish tank. It is important for teachers to have their young students experience a variety of evaporation investigations in science class and stress that the water does not disappear but enters another phase called water vapor.

The fifth graders in this talk, Andrea and Joshua, proposed that the water was coming from the moisture in the air. Andrea already seemed to understand this at the beginning of the talk, but was not sure, evidenced by her offering many other ideas. By the end of the talk, I think she was convinced that the water was coming from the moisture in the air. At the beginning of the talk, Joshua said the water was coming from the ice when the heat melted it, but, when given an opportunity to evaluate his own ideas during the talk, he decided it had to come from moisture in the air.

When confronted with the question of why the water on the outside of the bottle was not blue, students were forced to evaluate their existing state of knowledge. If students know that water vapor exists in the air, they can come to the scientific conclusion that the water on the outside of the bottle is the water vapor that changed to the liquid phase. Students who do not know that water exists invisibly in the air in the form of water vapor pose a variety of other interesting explanations.

A very common naïve conception is what Kate, Ron, and Jim proposed, that of sweat. This word is used in our everyday language to describe similar phenomena, so it is not a surprise that many students use it for their explanation. Some students, like Jim, think the sweat is transferred from their hands, but when some of the other students' thinking is probed further, they seem to believe that inanimate objects function the same as living things. This concept is one that they will study later in biology.

Other students believe that there are very tiny microscopic holes in the container through which water can pass. With further probing, some say that the water can pass through the holes, but the color can't. If students propose this explanation, the teacher could guide students in proposing the question of what would happen to a similar container with blue water that is not frozen. When they discover the water does not condense on this bottle, then they might conclude that the phenomenon has something to do with the temperature. Then they may wonder at which temperature drops of water form. With some guidance, students could investigate the dew point.

I have learned so much more since that first science talk. Instead of telling students the correct explanation for condensation during or after the science talk, teachers can help students develop a deeper understanding by engaging them in activities such as I have just described. Learning to implement a science talk has helped me do what is recommended by the National Science Education Standards (NRC 1996), that is to: plan an inquiry-based science program; guide and facilitate student learning; assess teaching and student learning; develop an environment that enables students to learn science; create a community of learners; and plan and develop a school science program.

Reflections

The author of this chapter provides an example of teacher research from a teacher who is well along in a doctoral program and whose experience with writing academic prose and whose comfort with theoretical frameworks are evident. Monica writes, "While transcribing the children's responses, I found there were many ideas that I missed during the talk. By reflecting on those ideas that I heard as well as the ideas that I missed, I am thinking about ways that I could improve my facilitation of science talks." Taping and transcribing are activities more often found within the sphere of the researcher than that of the teacher, but, when Monica transcribes, her identity as a teacher is central to the experience. She is thinking about how to improve her teaching. In our spectrum of teacher research, this chapter includes a more theoretical perspective and more detailed analysis of student conversation, but it is as firmly grounded in classroom practice as the other chapters.

The science talk Monica reports here is accessible and interesting. The way that she documents and interprets her experience with the children shows how conducting research helps teachers understand and develop their practice. She is a teacher, speaking to other teachers, and at the same time contributing to the research community.

References

Brown, A. L., and A. S. Palincsar. 1989. Guided, cooperative learning and individual knowledge acquisition. In *Knowing, learning, and instruction: Essays in honor of Robert Glasser,* ed. L. Resnick. Mahwah, NJ: Lawrence Erlbaum.

Collins, A., J. S. Brown, and A. Holum.1991. Cognitive apprenticeship: Making thinking visible. *American Educator,* Winter: 6–11, 38–46.

Duckworth, E. R. 1996. *The having of wonderful ideas and other essays on teaching and learning,* 2nd ed. New York: Teachers College Press.

Gallas, K. 1995. *Talking their way into science: Hearing children's questions and theories, responding with curricula.* New York: Teachers College Press.

Teacher Research

Latour, B., and S. Woolgar. 1986. *Laboratory life: The construction of scientific facts,* 2nd ed. Princeton, NJ: Princeton University Press.

Linn, M. C., and S. Hsi. 2000. *Computers, teachers, peers: Science learning partners.* Mahwah, NJ: Lawrence Erlbaum.

National Research Council (NRC). 1996. *National Science Education Standards.* Washington, DC: National Academy Press.

Vygotsky, L. S. 1978. *Mind in society: The development of higher psychological processes.* Cambridge, MA: Harvard University Press.

Wood, D., J. S. Bruner, and G. Ross 1976. The role of tutoring in problem solving. *Journal of Child Psychiatry and Psychology* 17: 89–100.

Ongoing Studies of Learning and Teaching in Science Contexts

Teachers are ideally placed to carry out long-term inquiries. This set of case studies represents the wide variety of ways that teachers can approach and report such research. These authors explore some of the deeper issues that surround students' lives and learning. While teaching science, they have been able to think about their students in more global ways. Ellen Franz uses the genre of poetry to reflect upon conversations she had over an extended time period with a second-grade African American student about his future. In a year-long inquiry conducted as a master's project, a special educator, Mary Bell, documents the progress of a quiet student who rarely participated in class. Matthew Ronfeldt reports his research findings about the evolving ethical perspectives of his eighth-grade science students over the school year. Also reflecting upon a long-term experience, a mentor teacher and student teacher, Claire Bove and Matthew Reider, tell stories about ways in which they learned from one another and their students while teaching middle school science.

Jonathan

Ellen Franz

Ellen Franz is a teacher at an elementary school in the Sausalito Marin City School District, a small district just north of San Francisco. When she wrote this poem, she was teaching primary grades in a midsized urban school district and had been in education for 17 years. She is a poet who achieves, through her poetry, the kind of understanding that reaches from deep inside a teacher to deep inside a student. Her poem shows how reflections on teaching and learning can include more than studies of curriculum, assessment, and standards.

As a white, female educator working primarily with African American students, I am learning to build bridges between my own and my students' cultural backgrounds as we strive toward achievement of academic excellence. At the time I wrote this piece, my teacher research work revolved around learning to build bridges between my own more analytic learning and teaching style and my students' more relational learning style (Cohen 1969). The poem is a snapshot of an ongoing conversation a student and I had over the course of several months, months in which I was tracking my use of conversation to help students build connections between content work and their own lives—past, present, and future. You can meet some of my students and read about my continued work in this area on my website: Personal Geometries: Working Within the Variable Landscapes of Language, Culture, Curriculum and Relationship: *http://gallery. carnegiefoundation.org/collections/quest/collections/sites/franz_ellen.*

I—June 2000

"I like Engineering,"
you say
one recess,
staying in,
trying to figure out how to make the car
you've built
run faster.

"Well," I say,
looking at you,
"you should start thinking
about college. Engineers
go to college."

"But Ms. Franz!"
you respond,
screwing up your eyes
tight,
looking at me through slits,
brow furrowed,
"I'm only in the second grade!"

"It's never too soon to
start thinking, Jonathan."

"I shouldn't haf'ta think
about college 'til
at least
junior high!"

II—A few days later

Again, you are refining
your vehicle design.

I am sitting nearby.

"I don't gotta go to college
to build things," you say,
"I can make money
just building things."

"Yep," I say, "that's true.
The architects and engineers
will tell you what to build
and you can build it.
They make more money, though."

"They do?"

III—The next day

This time
you have a book in your hands
ready to put away.

You turn,
say to me,

"When I'm an engineer,
I'm gonna get me a
really tight car."

IV—A few weeks later

Something leads me to
mention college.

You and Rashawn are
sitting on desks
after school.

You lean back
and announce,
"I ain't goin' to college.
Gonna be a waste o' my time."

"Why do you think that,
Jonathan?"

"I just know. Ain't goin'
to high school neither.
Just be a waste o' my time…

I want one o' those degrees from…"
You trail off, look at me, try again,

"I want one o' those degrees
from…"

"Junior high?" I fill in, unsure,
questioning.

"Yeah. That's it. Junior high.
My uncle's got one o' those."

V—For months after

Each time the words
high school or
college
come out of my mouth
in your presence,
you almost shout,

"I'm not goin'!"

When I tell your mom this,
laughter in my voice,
she says to me,
a smile in her eyes,

"He's just trying to get
your attention."

VI—February 2001

This particular day
our class has begun to
learn
"The Dream Keepers,"
by Langston Hughes.

You have already stood
in front of the class
presenting
the almost-memorized poem
to us.
(You only needed a little help.)

After school
this day,
you are on the phone,
then waiting,
then on the phone,
hoping for a ride home.

I am standing,
reading the entry about
Langston Hughes
from the big *Africana* book.

I read you bits and pieces
in between your
phone calls.

Before we leave,
I say to you,
"Wait. Let me read you
my other favorite poem
by Langston Hughes."

"O.K.," you say,
pulling chairs down from
desk tops,

one for each of us.

We sit.

I read.

Mother to Son

Well, son, I'll tell you:
Life for me ain't been no crystal stair.
It's had tacks in it,
And splinters,
And boards torn up,
And places with no carpet on the floor—
     Bare.
     But all the time

I'se been a-climbin' on,
And reachin' landin's,
And turnin' corners,
And sometimes goin' in the dark
Where there ain't been no light.
So, boy, don't you turn back.
Don't you set down on the steps
'Cause you finds it kinder hard.
Don't you fall now—
For I'se still goin', honey,
I'se still climbin',
And life for me ain't been no crystal stair.

When I stop reading,
you say,
quietly,
forcefully,

"Wow.
I really like that."

Then there is quiet for a moment,
no words
between us,

a full silence
just for a moment.

Then you say,
and I will never forget this,

"I guess I gotta go to college, hunh."
                    —Ellen Franz

Reflections

Collecting evidence and making sense of the evidence are two elements of teacher research. Ellen is a poet, and one of the tools of the poet is a journal in which words are stored up for later use. In the previous chapter, we saw that Monica's identity as a teacher was integral to her identity as a researcher. Ellen's poem shows us that her identity as a teacher is integral to her identity as a poet. She is collecting student words, not with a tape recorder, but with her poet's ear. When she makes sense of these words, it is with her poet's sensibility. Her data collection and sense making result in a research report in the form of a work of art.

As a primary teacher, Ellen's teaching practice includes teaching engineering, teaching literature, making personal connections with her students and their families, understanding how to motivate her students, and thinking about the whole child—past, present, and future. How is a primary teacher able to be the science department, English language arts specialist, counselor, social worker, and caring friend all at once? Only by being all these people at the same time.

Reference

Cohen, R. 1969. Conceptual styles, culture conflict, and nonverbal tests of intelligence. *American Anthropologist New Series* 71(5): 828–856.

Chapter 6

When Students Don't Talk: Searching for Reasons

Mary P. Bell

Mary Bell has taught for 23 years in a large suburban school district near Washington, DC. As an elementary special education and Reading Recovery teacher, she cotaught reading, science, and math as part of an inclusion model. Currently, she is working as a special education instructional specialist within the Department of Curriculum and Instruction of this district. Mary used student records, videotapes, audiotapes, student work, her own reflective journal notes, and observational tallies taken by an aide to understand a puzzling silence on the part of one of her students. This study documents Mary's inquiry into the source of her student's silence and shows how teachers and families working together can help a silent student find his voice.

Elementary school classrooms are busy places. Teachers are involved with implementing vast curriculum in a given amount of time. They must think on their feet and make decisions quickly, often relying on student responses to guide their actions.

I teach at an elementary school in a suburb of Washington, DC. I am both a reading recovery teacher and a special educator. In order to serve the children with individualized education plans more effectively, I am coteaching in the fourth grade in the areas of science, reading, and mathematics.

I have been an educator for 23 years. During that time, there have been several students I will term "The Silent Ones." These students rarely talk in class. Some appear to be talkative during lunch, recess, or physical education (PE). Others have parents who report during conference time that their children are rarely quiet at home and in fact report everything that goes on at school down to the last detail. The students are not necessarily receiving special education services. It is difficult, however, to assess what these students know due to the lack of verbal feedback a teacher receives.

Puzzlements

For the past three years, I had noticed a boy I will refer to as Jose. I had rarely seen Jose talk. While I was coteaching in his second-grade classroom, I noticed he spoke only when spoken to. Additionally, I had had lunch duty with Jose's grade levels for second, third, and fourth grades. I had never observed him talk to other students during lunch. I was coteaching Jose's fourth-grade class in the subjects of reading, science, and math, and I hadn't seen him raise his hand to answer any questions, although in written form he was capable of producing average work. Why did Jose rarely speak? What could I do to encourage his participation without turning it into a grade? If I encouraged talking in one subject area, would it overflow into others? Was English a second language for Jose? How was education viewed in his household, and what, if any, supports were there? Was oral communication present in his home environment? These were the questions I sought to answer.

Record Review

I was curious about Jose's quietness and thought that, perhaps in his records, I would find a clue. I first checked Jose's attendance card and noticed that he had attended our school since kindergarten. The fact that he had been absent 23 days in the first grade caught my eye. There was a letter from the school expressing a concern over these absences but stating that he would be promoted to the second grade.

I then examined Jose's report cards. At the end of kindergarten, Jose had not mastered all kindergarten objectives. Indeed, he didn't know the numbers *0, 4, 6, 7, 9,* and *10.* He did not know the color *green.* He could count orally to 14 and knew all of his upper-case letters but only 24 of his lower-case letters. The teacher's comment in June stated:

> Jose has progressed well through the year. However, he continues to struggle in many reading and language skills. Continue to work with Jose on his reading and language skills. Work on his sight words as he continues to read through the summer.

I also noticed a referral to our School Instructional Team during his kindergarten year. The teacher indicated that Jose was quiet and would not volunteer information. When called on, he would reply, "I don't know." The PE and music teachers also commented that Jose seldom spoke but would perform the tasks they asked him to do.

In first grade, Jose was below grade level in reading and received reading recovery services. Comments reflected upon his below-grade-level skills and that retention was being considered.

By second grade, Jose's report card indicated "progressing satisfactorily." The teacher noted below-grade-level skills and the need to improve written communication.

Jose's third-grade report card was As and Bs with the only comment indicating below-grade-level skills in reading. For the first time, his parents did not show up for any conferences.

So far, it seemed that reading was always a concern. Oral communication was not Jose's strong point and in fact was a concern to his kindergarten teacher. Yet, he continued to receive good grades. What was it about Jose that worried some of his teachers? Did his excellent behavior mask some true difficulties? Why was he absent in the first grade and what had happened during his reading recovery program? How had he managed to receive satisfactory report cards? I wanted to find out.

Oral Inquiry

I decided the best way to find out about Jose's past was to invite several of the people who knew him best to an oral discussion. On November 8, his mother, three fourth-grade teachers, the music teacher, a special educator, his reading recovery teacher, the school counselor, and I met to discuss Jose. I started the conversation by expressing my observation that Jose rarely spoke during school. After introductions, I asked his mother to start off by telling us about Jose's childhood. The following is a partial transcript of the meeting. "Teacher" refers to myself.

Mother: Jose was kind of slow when he was growing. I would think about two years he would start walking, maybe about one-and-one-half talking.

Teacher: So, he was talking before he was walking.

Mother: Yes and there were concerns and taking him back and forth to the doctors and getting scans—nothing came up. I mean, I guess it's just hereditary in the family. I was the same way. All through kindergarten through 12th grade, I was the same way. I was shy, wouldn't participate, wouldn't raise my hand. When I had to get in front of the class, I would duck my head down in order to read the report and would never look up in front of the class. I just think it's hereditary. There's no physical or mental problems with him.

At this point in the conversation, I couldn't help but think of the article I had read the night before. Jere Brophy (1996) stated that some children have not developed effective communication skills because their parents seldom converse with them or respond positively to their verbal initiations. Additionally, they have not had much contact with peers. The conversation continued.

Teacher: Well, is he shy at home? I mean how is he at home with the family and people that he really knows?

Reading recovery teacher: Like with his cousins. I remember we talked about that years ago.

Mother He is open to them.

Teacher: Is he whooping and hollering like they are?

Mother: He's more active, more playful. I notice that when I scold him or raise my voice to a certain tone, he ducks his head and start to cry. He's very easily sensitive.

At this point, I realized that Jose seemed to be quiet both at home and at school, although he did not qualify as being socially phobic. In those instances, children exhibit such extreme shyness that it interferes with things that children normally do, such as make friends, play, participate in class, and even attend school (Rueter 2000). His mother, also quiet and shy, appeared to blame heredity for Jose's quietness. Lynne Kelly, a shyness expert, concurs that shyness has two causes, nature and nurture (Education World, n.d.). Jose's mother appeared to support this theory. The conversation progressed and the discussion focused on Jose's life outside of school. Jose did not mention anyone at school with whom he was friendly. His neighborhood friends, interestingly enough, were both students who received special education services. They were both sixth-grade students and very outgoing, talkative children.

Jose's reading teacher noticed that although Jose would not raise his hand, he would answer a question when asked. The conversation continued in much the same way. The music teacher, who also had the advantage of knowing Jose's older sister and two younger brothers, was not overly concerned with Jose's quietness. His reading recovery teacher mentioned how difficult it was to teach Jose because he would not talk. Part of a reading recovery lesson is to engage the student in conversation and then to write a sentence. I asked about his progress in reading recovery and whether or not he had been successfully discontinued. His teacher told me that, due to his extended absence from the country, he was exited from the program. I was curious about Jose's absences in first grade and decided to ask about those. His mother told us that the family had visited extended family in Mexico. I also found out that Jose does not speak Spanish nor is Spanish spoken in the home.

His present fourth-grade teachers were not concerned about Jose's lack of conversation. Indeed, I got the sense they thought I was being overly concerned about Jose. He was quiet, obeyed the rules, and completed his work. Why would I want more?

The conversation did not seem to be reaching any conclusions. Realizing that, if Jose's lack of conversation were due to anxiety, he would not outgrow it without some type of intervention (Workman 1999), I decided to force the team to take action, whether or not all of the team members thought Jose needed to talk. I decided to ask outright what we all thought we could do to increase Jose's conversation. If I wanted him to talk in science class, it made sense to me to encourage conversation in all subject areas. We decided on a plan of action:

Teacher Research

1. Because Jose's main delight appeared to be soccer, we would ask the PE teacher to use Jose as an aide as often as possible. (The PE teacher often used fourth-grade students as aides for teaching the kindergarten and first-grade classes.)
2. I would talk to Jose and let him know we wanted him to participate more in class. I felt that he should be let in on the plan.
3. All three fourth-grade teachers would use Jose as a messenger as much as possible. Because the fourth grade is departmentalized, Jose is taught by all of the teachers.
4. Jose would meet with a first-grade child, who desperately needed someone to talk to, three times a week, for 15 minutes. We hoped this would make it possible for both children to meet faculty goals.
5. Mrs. B, a teacher's aide working with the fourth grade, would keep a tally chart. This chart would reflect how often Jose raised his hand.

Tracking Progress

As suggested by our plan of action, I held a casual conversation with Jose in which I told him that I had noticed he rarely spoke during school. I explained to him that this often made it difficult for his teachers to know how much he understood. I encouraged him to talk more in school, particularly during science talks.

I decided to keep a journal in which I would note Jose's progress. I hoped to record changes in behavior as well as any milestones.

September 26, 2001—Jose raised his hand for the first time in math class today. I praised him for offering his answer—although it was incorrect.

October 22, 2001—Jose actually raised his hand at lunch today. He told me he had a job on Sunday working with his cousin at a car wash.

November 13, 2001—Mrs. D, Jose's social studies teacher, told me she's noticed an increase in Jose's oral participation since the oral inquiry group. I arranged for Jose to start talking with Casey (a pseudonym) tomorrow. There has been no change in science and math (Bell 2002).

Additionally, I was holding video- and audiotaped discussions during science. In these discussions, students orally discussed scientific questions. As of December 1, we had discussed such questions as: "What makes wind?" "What makes a full Moon?" and "What makes rain?" To date, Jose had not said anything during these discussions, although he had provided written comments on his opinion.

October 31, 2001—What makes a full Moon? Jose: I think it is number 2 [copied from the board]. It is light from the Sun because the Sun shines on the Moon.

November 9, 2001: What makes rain? Jose: I dis [disagree] with Herry's [Henry's] because their [there] might be mare [more] in the Lake [lake].

Jose's written language skills did not reflect grade-level expectations. It was my hope to see an improvement in his writing as we observed an improvement in his oral language skills.

After a fourth-grade team meeting I learned from his teacher's remarks that Jose appeared to orally participate in social studies. Because I did not coteach in this subject area, I decided to observe the classroom and learning style of the teacher. What was it about the culture of the classroom that made Jose more comfortable and willing to speak? The following is an excerpt from my observation. *(S) Teacher* refers to the social studies teacher.

(S) Teacher began to read the chapter and paraphrased the context of every other sentence.

(S) Teacher: What's happening in the picture of the settlement of Jamestown?

Ann: People working, taking cows in.

(S) Teacher: What else? What have they done?

Travis: Umm...

(S) Teacher: What do you think? Did they just get off of the boat and everything was there?

Donnie: Cut down trees, built houses.

Nate: They are doing chores.

(S) Teacher: What do you see in the background?

Jose's hand is raised.

Ann: It looks like there's lots of trees, houses.

The teacher moved through her lessons slowly and deliberately, rephrasing whenever a new concept was being taught. If the students were listening and paying attention, they would be able to answer the questions the teacher asked.

Pondering my observation, I realized the classroom culture was very nurturing. The teacher provided the necessary scaffolding for student success. Materials, in this case the text, were readily accessible.

How could I restructure science class to encourage Jose's participation? Would the strides he made in social studies class increase his participation in other subject areas? Would his conversations with the first-grade student increase his own participation? Would further research on my own and with my fellow teachers shine any light on these puzzlements?

Mid-Year Reflection

During the month of January, I continued my journal writing. The following are revealing excerpts.

January 2, 2002—Jose was named Student of the Month for December!

January 11, 2002—Jose volunteered two times during science!

January 17, 2002—The fourth-grade team met as scheduled. I had a chance to update the team, and they me, on Jose. He continues to volunteer during "Popcorn Reading." Additionally, as reported by Mrs B, he volunteers at least once a period. Math is sporadic but he participates.

January 16, 2002—I had a revelation! After our team meeting, I realized that the day Jose volunteered in science was the day we read a text as a whole class. When I observed his social studies class, it was the same situation. Perhaps he is an auditory learner.

January 23, 2002—Jose raised his hand and talked during our science talk today. We were talking about static electricity and balloons. He said he thought the balloons would not be attracted to one another if we rubbed two balloons on material and then we laid them down.

Teacher: So, sometimes magnets have different poles or different sides? Anyone else have an opinion? How are these going? Yeah, Jose?

Jose: I think, 'cause I tried it, um, they didn't stick together. The balloons didn't stick together.

Teacher: OK. So, you're agreeing. You saw the same thing as Elly. When you tried it, they repel.

I bought Jose an ice cream at lunch!

January 29, 2002—Miss C came to me very excited during lunch. Apparently Jose had his hand up for every question today during health. When asked a question, he responded correctly four times. I then asked if they had been reading a text in class. She replied, "Yes." This confirms my observation of when Jose is animated (Bell 2002).

At this point, I reread material on the website Science Education for Hispanic Students (n.d.). Although Jose did not speak Spanish, I knew he heard it. I wanted to know if this had an impact on his oral participation. The article made three important suggestions. The first was to invite students to talk about topics with which they are familiar, connecting our lesson plans to their prior knowledge. Second, the authors suggested communicating realistic expectations for these students throughout the school year. Third, they suggested using cognitive coaching to help promote critical thinking skills by asking students who have correctly answered a problem "How did you get that? Why?"

After observing and working closely with all of Jose's teachers, I felt the teachers involved with Jose had dealt with the first two points. I decided to observe Jose closely during reading instruction, paying attention to the questions he answered. Interestingly enough, his second period report card comment stated: "Jose is contributing more and more in reading group. He should be reading outside of class (Book It) and writing a brief paragraph about what he read. Please continue to encourage this at home."

On February 5, 2002, I had the opportunity to share my study of Jose with a group of colleagues who were pursuing puzzlements of their own. One of their suggestions was to track the type of questions Jose answers. Were they factual questions? Had the answers been clearly present in the reading? Would he respond to "higher-level thinking" questions, which require more thought and a higher degree of risk taking? As I had these same puzzlements, I decided it was time to observe.

Research and Reflection

Before I observed Jose, I decided I needed to research scaffolding and the effects on teaching and thus students. My colleagues' questions I felt, directly related to how much and what kind of support Jose needed to answer questions. Chuck Sandy (1999) put things succinctly when he wrote:

> The teacher must anticipate in advance not only which learners are likely to collapse, but also in what ways. This, of course, requires in-depth knowledge of the learners' needs, strengths, and weaknesses as well as the experience to know just when to take away, replace, or add support.

Scaffolding is central to social constructivists' theories of learning (Roehler and Cantion 1996). Scaffolding occurs during social interactions between students and teachers that precedes internalization of knowledge. For this to occur, the teacher carefully gears instruction, through conversations, toward topics that have educational value. Background information is sought and discussed and the teacher guides the students toward new levels of understanding. The teacher is the facilitator of oral and written discourse. This information underscored the importance of oral student participation in class.

Jose's mother was called in to our School Improvement Team on March 11 to discuss Jose's brother. She revealed that she and her husband had been separated since last year. This had not come up during our oral inquiry, perhaps due to her shy nature and the embarrassment of the event. I suggested to the school counselor that she work with Jose and his three siblings in a group to help with this crisis. Although Jose appeared to be dealing with the situation, his two brothers were having a difficult time. The counselor agreed. His mother also relayed to me that Jose was talking more at home. This validated the proactive approach described in *The Shy Child* (Zimbardo 1999). The author suggests making a conscious plan to help the child overcome shyness—both at home and at school. I decided not to ask Mom in for another midyear inquiry group because she had had to take time off from work for this meeting.

On March 20, 2002, I observed Jose during reading instruction. I asked the teacher to probe Jose with a variety of questions in order that I might observe which types of questions he was answering. It became clear, quite quickly, that Jose was responding to detail questions. When the teacher asked a question that could be answered from a picture or from the reading, Jose raised his hand. He avoided inference questions and appeared to have some trouble making predictions. When the teacher asked *why* questions or *what do you think* questions, Jose did not raise his hand. If called on, he remained silent. According to Diana Masny (1995) in her article "Literacy Development in Young Children," there are three interactions that promote oral literate behavior. The students are read to orally and both reader and students discuss the contents orally by

- Asking questions and making simple comments concerning labels of objects,
- Asking questions that require more detailed information about objects, and
- Asking questions that require the child to elaborate on aspects of events, discuss motives and explore causes.

In the successive interactions, the child is asked:

- To evaluate or react to information in "texts" and
- To relate events in "texts" to the real world (Masny 1995, p. 5).

Once again, careful scaffolding of information appeared to be a necessary ingredient of success. I suggested to the teacher that next time, she offer Jose three possible answers to choose from when he seemed unable to respond.

That same day I was teaching math to his class. I presented the following question:

Mrs. Bell bought lemon/limeade for a party. She wanted to make 5 pkgs. How much water would she need?

Pkgs	1	2	3	4	5
Cups	2	4	6	8	10

Explain how you got your answer.

Jose wrote, "I counted by ones and then I counted by twos. Mrs. Bell needed 10 cups of water." The bold numbers in the chart indicate Jose's response.

He was one of three students in a class of 24 to explain his answer correctly. He was the only student to write that Mrs. Bell would need 10 cups of water as part of his answer. I had been modeling the process of answering word problems and correctly writing a summarizing sentence all year, four times a week. Jose was showing progress in certain areas, and those areas appeared to be where scaffolding had occurred.

On March 22, I asked the first-grade teacher how the conversations were going between Jose and her student. In fact, her student had been identified as having attention-deficit/hyperactivity disorder (ADHD) and was now on medication. The conversations with Jose had dwindled as her student had less need to talk and express his feelings. As I had been noticing Jose talking more during lunch, I decided to let the matter drop and concentrate more on altering instruction to promote Jose's participation.

Mrs. B, an aide who was tallying Jose's conversations, had to go on medical leave unexpectedly for six weeks beginning the end of March. This effort, though important, was not fruitful. She had tallied only the times when Jose raised his hand and was called on. She did not record how many times he raised his hand. Before her leave, however, tally marks were on the rise.

Dec.	Jan.	Feb.	March
5	7	14	22

On March 23, we had another science talk discussion. The question asked was "What makes a full Moon?" Although this question had been discussed in October, we had not reached a conclusion. Jose did not speak but he did record a written belief.

Before the talk: I think the rain and the clouds make a full Moon.

After the talk: I agree with number 3 (referring to a drawing on the board) because the Sun is getting light to the Moon.

Jose's writing supports the need for scaffolding. In this case, it was in the form of a scientific inquiry discussion.

Jose's mother attended a conference for his brother on April 3. I had the opportunity to ask her how Jose was doing at home.

Mother: Oh, he is talking much more at home.
Teacher: That's great!
Mother: I even have him in soccer, for three weeks now. I've put all the boys in. Jose's doing well.

Teacher Research

Teacher: I remember that he always plays soccer at recess. That's great. He is talking much more here at school as well (Bell 2002).

I was delighted to hear that Jose was conversing more both at home and at school. I couldn't help but remember our plan to have Jose help the PE teacher with equipment. Now, his mother had signed him up for a soccer team. I was very excited.

On April 12, the teachers were given a day to hold conferences and work on report cards. Much to my dismay, I learned that Jose's grades had fallen in most subject areas, mainly due to not turning in homework on a consistent basis. We quickly arranged for a parent conference on April 18. I encouraged Jose's mother to allow Jose to be present at the conference.

On April 18, the conference was held, with Jose's mother, his fourth-grade teachers, and me. Jose was unable to attend because his father had taken him and his two brothers on a trip to New York. Jose's mother revealed that she knew Jose's grades were falling in school. As a single mother—a grandmother was also in the home—Jose's mother was giving her efforts to Jose's younger brothers, who were having great difficulties and were being considered for retention. As a group, we brainstormed for ways to support Jose. He hadn't been turning in his homework. How could we encourage him to do so? Then one of the teachers remarked on his behavior in class.

Mrs. V: Now on the flip side of this, he has become very social.
Teacher: That's good.
Mrs. V: It's kind of what we're working toward; however, he still can't distinguish when it is appropriate or not.

The conference resulted in a plan of action. Mom would check his homework and set aside 30 minutes each night if Jose needed help. At school, we would make sure Jose turned in his work by eliciting the help of the teacher's aide. In addition, I would speak to Jose about the Treasure Chest reward and to his counselor to ask her to address the subject of appropriate times for speaking during one of her sessions with Jose.

The next day, I spoke with Jose about the Treasure Chest reward system. He was very enthusiastic. I also spoke to the counselor. She told me that the sessions with Jose and his brothers were progressing nicely. Jose had no trouble talking to her, nor with his brothers. She said she'd be happy to address the appropriate times to converse during school. I warned her not to be too harsh on them, because I didn't want our efforts to backfire.

In science, we were beginning a new unit on rocks. Each child had to collect 12 rocks. We later weighed each rock. The children got to choose one special rock. Jose's special rock was heart shaped. I asked him to tell me about it.

Jose: Well, it's shaped like a heart. That's why I picked it.
Teacher: Do you know what kind it is?
Jose: [Silence]
Teacher: Well, let's look at the chart and the descriptions of the three types.

Jose and I read the chart together. When we had finished, he quickly and correctly labeled his rock as sedimentary rock. This confirmed my belief that, when children who have difficulty verbalizing are given choices, they are able to answer with ease.

Knowing how important it was for Jose to hear about his accomplishments, I went outside at recess with Jose and his classmates. I mentioned on the way outside how proud I was of his accomplishments. He was talking more in class, completing his homework, and receiving good grades for his efforts. He politely replied, "thank you," but it was his large smile that said it all.

Final Efforts and Results

As a result of the oral inquiries, team meetings, and various conversations held regarding Jose, the fourth-grade team became sensitive to other students who did not orally participate in class and started forming plans to include some of these students with Jose in special "responsibilities." For example, a female of Asian descent was paired with Jose to help raise the flag each morning.

Jose's mother, through various conversations with the school, has made strides in supporting our efforts at school. Talking to Jose to support speaking in school, enrolling him in soccer, and monitoring his homework at home depict these efforts.

Helping the PE teacher, serving as class messenger, and talking with the first-grade student appeared to be enjoyable tasks for Jose. Occasionally, he would raise his hand during lunch to tell me an anecdote concerning one of these special jobs.

Jose improved the extent of his conversation and his writing ability at school. This was evident not only through tally marks and observations but also through his class work, homework, report card grades, and teacher comments.

Teachers need to be reminded how important proper scaffolding becomes to students, particularly students who rarely speak in class. I shared this with the fourth-grade team, and I asked to speak at a staff meeting to address this issue and to provide a handout about my enlightenments stemming from my teacher research. (See Appendix 1.)

The Future

What would the next year hold for Jose? Would our efforts be fruitful in fifth grade as well as future grades? Time would tell. My hope was that, through teacher awareness, Jose and students like him would continue to be nurtured, that through teacher planning, his learning would continue and Jose would reach his full potential.

Appendix 1

Strategies for Helping Shy or Withdrawn Children Who Rarely Speak
1. Encourage peer involvement. Examples: Cross-age tutoring, group games, cooperative learning opportunities.
2. Adjust student seating. Examples: Sit next to friendly children, near the teacher, near their friends.
3. Minimize stress and embarrassment. Examples: Talk privately about your goal to have them orally participate; arrange a private signal as to when you will call on them; when their hands are raised reinforce this effort.
4. Engage the students in special activities. Examples: Class messenger, Student of the Month.
5. Provide scaffolding for learning activities. Examples: Call on them when asking review questions; give them a choice between two answers if they seem "stuck"; pass out an interest survey or hold a parent conference to gather student interests and activities—refer to these as you teach new material; if possible, connect lessons to the "real world."
6. Provide information on social insight. Examples: Suggest ways to initiate contact; explain that making friends may be hard at first; teach social "door openers."
7. Make time to talk to the student each day.
8. Display their good artwork or assignments.
9. Use "wait time." Allow all students to think about or write their answers before eliciting oral responses.
10. Privately, help students set goals for improving their communications. Example: Say to the student: "Try and ask questions in class tomorrow."
11. Establish good communications between home and school.
12. Provide positive feedback for improvements.

Reflections

All of the elements of teacher research are present in Mary's story about Jose: questioning ("puzzlements"), collecting evidence, making sense of the evidence, and sharing. There is an iterative nature to her use of these elements that teachers will recognize as a characteristic of good teaching practice. Mary wonders, consults the literature, collects data, makes sense of the data, talks with colleagues, wonders again, and continues to cycle through these elements as she tries to understand why Jose is silent and how to help him break out of his silence. In the middle of this story she writes, "Pondering my observation, I realized the classroom 'culture' was very nurturing. The teacher provided the necessary scaffolding for student success: How can I restructure science class to encourage Jose's participation? Will strides made in social studies class increase his participation in other subject areas? Will his conversations with the first-grade student increase his own participation? Will further research on my own and with my fellow teachers shine any light on these puzzlements?" These are the kinds of observations and questions that often guide teachers. What is unusual here is that Mary has recorded the process so carefully that other teachers can learn from what she has done.

References

Bell, M. P. 2001–2002. My personal journal.

Brophy, J. 1996, November. Working with shy or withdrawn students (*Eric* Identifier: ED402070). Available online at: *www.eric.ed.gov* Retrieved July 24, 2006, from this new address for ERIC documents.

Education World. n.d. How can teachers help shy students? Interview with Lynne Kelly. Retrieved January 30, 2002, from *www.education-world.com/a_curr/curr267.shtml*.

Masny, D. 1995. Literacy development in young children [Electronic Version]. *Interaction, Canadian Child Care Federation,* Spring, 1995. Retrieved March 12, 2002, from *www.cfc-efc.ca/docs/cccf/00000049.htm*.

Roehler, L. R., and D. J. Cantion. 1996, May 10. *Scaffolding: A powerful tool in social constructivist classrooms* [Electronic Version] Retrieved March 12, 2002, from *http://ed-web3.educ.msu.edu/Literacy/papers/paperlr2.htm*.

Rueter, J. 2000, February 24. University of Maryland study shows socially phobic children can "come out of their shells." University of Maryland Press Release. Retrieved January 30, 2002, from *www.inform.umd.edu/CampusInfo/Depa...nstAdv/newsdesk/releases/2000/00024r.html* (not found, July 24, 2006).

Sandy, C. 1999. *The teacher as builder and architect. The Language Teacher Online 23:06.* Retrieved March 12, 2002, from a URL no longer working, Retrieved July 24, 2006, from a new URL: *www.jalt-publications.org/tlt/articles/1999/06/sandy*.

Science Education for Hispanic Students website: Retrieved November 4, 2001, from *www.as.wvu.edu/~equity/hispanic.html*.

Workman, B. 1999, February 11. Center for Anxiety Disorders opens at University of Maryland. University of Maryland press release. Retrieved January 30, 2002, from *www.inform.umd.edu/CampusInfo/Depa...nstAdv/newsdesk/releases/1999/99016r.html* (not found July 24, 2006).

Zimbardo, P. G. 1999. *The shy child.* Cambridge, MA: Institute for the Study of Human Knowledge, Malor Books.

Evolving Ethical Perspectives in an Eighth-Grade Science Classroom

Matthew Ronfeldt

Matthew Ronfeldt's dissertation as a doctoral candidate in Curriculum and Teacher Education at Stanford University is a crossprofessional study of how professional education supports novice teachers and clinical psychologists in adapting to their new professional roles. He wrote this chapter while teaching eighth-grade math and science at a school in the San Francisco Bay area, where he developed and coordinated a teacher research group within the school. He received his MA in education from Mills College, where he also participated as a teacher researcher for three years. Matt used videotapes of class discussions, interviews, student work, and his own reflections to study, over the course of the school year, the developing ideas of his students as they explored the ethical issues facing those who conduct scientific experiments. As his students debated whether and when it is acceptable to do experiments on animals or humans, they stated their opinions, they challenged each other, and they changed their minds. Matt provided opportunities for scientific discussion and debate, nurtured a classroom climate where students shared responsibility for learning, and modeled inquiry in his own practice as he encouraged his students to ask their own questions.

Setting the Context: The Big Questions Underneath the Smaller Ones

I went into teaching for moral, even spiritual reasons. Like so many other teachers entering the profession, education appealed to me because it provided the possibility for change in our society. Not change like the dot.com revolution that whirled around me, enticing my peers further into the culture of profit. Rather, change that might push minds to dig deeper into the heart and spirit. I went into teaching because of my belief that the path to happiness is paved by learning, not consumerism, and because of the potential for compassion and care to be harvested in the classroom.

To pursue this classroom vision, I sought out and found a first-year teaching position in a school that encouraged the exploration of ethical and moral questions in an eighth-grade integrated math and science classroom. Despite having this institutional support, I found exploring such ethical issues in class proved more complex than it seemed at first. There was not enough time to fully explore ethical topics on top of the curriculum that already existed. I considered downplaying many of the academic expectations around me—pressures to cover certain math topics and to prepare students for high school placement tests—so I could make a priority of ethical questions instead. However, this seemed to be a disservice to my students. They should be prepared to place out of algebra, for example, if they hoped to enter the honors track in high school. I found a potential solution in Parker Palmer's writings on the "embedded curricula." In his paper "Evoking the Spirit," Palmer (1999) proposes that the curricula that we already teach are replete with moral and spiritual questions. Our job as educators is to help students pull out these more meaningful lessons hidden inside the present curriculum. My research project is, at its core, an effort to bring Palmer's vision alive: How could I teach ethical/moral education embedded in my math and science classroom?

Ethical Flip-Flops

My research focus began to take shape during the first unit of the year, the "Brain and Learning Unit." Before covering the curriculum on how and why we learn and the connection between learning and our brains, I had all students write about their personal learning theories: (1) What is the purpose of learning? and (2) What is the purpose of school? This year I decided to hold onto their papers so I could return them after the unit was over. I thought it would be interesting to have them assess for themselves how their ideas had changed, if at all, over the course of the unit.

One student, John, began the year with a logic common among his peers:

We learn to get As, to do well in school, to get into a good college, to have more options and success (wealth) in life so that we will have more comfort and less stress in the future.

School and learning served a future purpose rather than having a present value in their own right. When John looked at his writing sample three months later, he began his written response, "I can't believe I wrote this at the beginning of the year!" He added that he believed that learning and school can be sources of pleasure and personal growth. He even questioned whether he had been in low spirits when he had completed this assignment. I considered numerous possible academic and social explanations for John's transformation. But the fact that such an extreme shift could occur in only three months, regardless of its causes, is what captivated me. I expected dramatic shifts in subject matter knowledge, but thought ethical and moral positions—like those related to the value and purpose of education—would be more deeply socialized and resistant to change.

Furthermore, it struck me that John was surprised that he had had these views at the beginning of the year. When reading his original writing sample, it were as though he had discovered somebody else's work, somebody whom he had never known before. John's transformation brought up two questions, in particular, for my teaching: Do students generally go through such extreme shifts with respect to ethical or philosophical views in such short periods of time? and Are they aware of their evolving perspectives?

John's ethical flip-flop inspired me to look more closely at how adolescents grapple with ethical questions over time. Thus, I decided that I wanted to pursue a specific ethical or spiritual question in the science curricula and follow student perspectives as we revisited it consistently throughout the year. Coincidentally, I assigned for homework an article about new developments in stem-cell research that elicited strong student reactions about the use of rats for research. During a heated class conversation about the article, one student posed the ethical question: "Why don't we breed humans or chimpanzees for science research?"

Parker Palmer came alive in my classroom, as students uprooted embedded ethical questions, questions on which I had not originally intended to focus. I did not need to add anything on top of the curriculum or force an ethical agenda upon them; I simply followed their ethical urges and built curricula and pedagogy around them—guiding walls for the class to consider their ethical dilemma. From September until June we revisited the same ethical questions through a variety of different reflective pedagogical approaches. The guiding classroom questions became: What are your perspectives on animal and human research? Under what conditions are such forms of research appropriate? Under what conditions are they inappropriate?

As I watched my students bend their minds around this theme throughout the year, I formed research questions to guide my own inquiry into their development: Through a series of continuous reflective science activities addressing a consistent ethical theme in science, will students be able to develop an ethical stance on the issue and will the stance evolve over time? If perspectives do evolve over time, are there common patterns for the trajectory of these developing perspectives? If not, what prevents students from developing and changing perspectives?

Methodology: Who and How I Would Research

Because I was interested in charting student perspectives over the course of the school year, I realized that it would be impossible to transcribe the views of all 48 adolescents. I chose instead to track six students in close detail, logging all written and verbal comments in and out of class that related to our central ethical focus on human and animal research. I chose six students according to three criteria:

- They demonstrated an authentic interest in the ethical questions,
- They were willing to volunteer their ideas frequently in either writing or conversation, and
- They started with different ethical stances from one another at the beginning of the year.

My reason for this last choice was based on literature suggesting that students within the same age group may exhibit widely different stages in ethical development (Hayes 1994, Walsh 2000). I thought it would be important to sample students from a variety of starting points, as I was interested in the development of all types of students.

The class confronted the ethical issue of human and animal research through unstructured written responses and in more structured written responses to video and reading assignments about real instances of these ethical issues in science research. An important example is the NOVA video "Secret of The Wild Child" (Garmon 1994) which I showed the class early in the year. This video documents the 1960's case of Genie—a teenage girl who had been locked in a closet by her abusive father until she was discovered by authorities at age 13. Scientists became interested in her as a rare case of human development and language acquisition without nurture. I had students write about whether they felt it was ethical for scientists to study this girl, even when they took personal responsibility for her care and upbringing.

Moreover, we had many classroom discussions about ethical issues in science as they related to reading, video, and personal anecdotes. Some of these classroom conversations were also videotaped and one was shown to students a few months later. The videotaped conversation was later used as a text to revisit the topic and as a means for students to reflect on their own perspectives. I also conducted and videotaped individual interviews at the end of the year with each research participant. All videotaped discussion and interviews were transcribed.

Preliminary Analysis:
The Gymnastics of Ethical Perspectives Unveiled

After collecting all of the data sets for each student, I compiled and chronologically organized all of their comments pertaining to our ethical focus. I then decided to use Lawrence Kohlberg's stage theory on moral development to try and categorize the ethical development and growth of the students. However, I had trouble fitting the student perspectives within Kohlberg's categorization of preconventional, conventional, and postconventional (Kohlberg 1969; Kroger 1996). [1]

After reading and rereading the transcriptions for any common themes or perspectives in students' views, I chose instead to use my own system of ethical classification. To make it simple for mapping, I created broad categories: individual prioritized (over science), neither prioritized, and science prioritized (over individual) (see Figure 1).

Figure 1: Classification of human research perspectives

Individual prioritized: The rights of the individual precede the interests of science research. Informed consent is required for all forms of research, both harmful and harmless. A person in this category may or may not support potentially lethal research in the case that subjects give informed consent.

Neither prioritized: The interests of science and the rights of the individual are in mutual conflict; the specific situation and the type of research determine which prevails. Informed consent may not be necessary for some harmless forms of research. Harmful and lethal forms of research are acceptable with informed consent, but not without it.

Science prioritized: The interests of science precede the rights of the individual. Consent is not required for research, even for some forms of harmful or lethal research.

This initial mapping of ethical development showed that the majority of students shifted classifications often and across the entire spectrum of my classification system. In fact, five out of six of the students took stances in all three classifications at some point during the year. I was surprised at how unstable and dynamic their ethical trajectories seemed. Their views bounced from one classification to the next with no clear pattern or sequence. Students were frequently torn between conflicting ethical stances, taking perspectives that would contradict previous ones, sometimes within the same comment. Only one student stayed within a single categorization throughout the year. This student took stances in every assignment and discussion that fell into the individual-prioritized classification; she never ventured into the other classifications even when peers challenged her views.

To illustrate the dramatic change in ethical stances that I generally observed, I present the cases of two students: James and Abbey. Moreover, I use these cases to demonstrate three common themes across my research participants: the important role of classroom conflict in ethical development, the ability to become more self-aware of one's own trajectory of ethical stances, and the ability to stabilize a particular stance over time.

James and His 12-Hour Transformation

James is an important case because of the dramatic shifts in perspective that he made in a short period of time. On March 8, I decided to show students footage of themselves from a videotaped ethical conversation that had occurred about four months prior. Before showing the video, I first had students reflect silently by prewriting about their past discussions and positions on these ethical topics. As a way to re-enter the ethical conversation and to push students to critically reflect on their own prior positions, I then showed 20 minutes of the videotaped classroom discussion from November 9. After reviewing this video segment, I asked students to discuss together their reactions to watching it and to share any thoughts about the ethical issues involved. That night, I assigned for homework a written reflection about the conversation from earlier that day. Because March 8 turned out to be one of the most significant days for James in terms of his ethical development, I am presenting chronologically some of the positions he took over approximately 12 hours:

1. *Prevideo write (March 8)*
   Q: What was your perspective on animal and human research at the beginning of the year?
   J: Of course it is cruel to test animals, but we are at the top of the food chain. God intended for us to take advantage of inferior races of animal, but he never wanted us to bring it upon ourselves. I think human testing is all bad. The only time it is okay is when we know for a fact that the experiments carried out will not harm our test subjects. For example, it is okay to do placebo testing. Not surgery testing. Anything is okay if the subject wants it.

2. *Postvideo discussion (March 8)*
   J: Well, I think that we should take inmates with death sentences and test them. I mean they are going to die eventually. They are going to get executed. I mean they might not even die by being tested but you might as well let them die with a good cause. Instead of just killing them uselessly, kill them with an experiment that saves humans or betters the human race. . . . Well, I don't really think it matters if they [death-row inmates] don't want to die or not.

3. Homework written reflection about class discussion (March 8)

Q: In the second paragraph, discuss which perspectives on human and animal research impacted you most and why? Which comments did you agree with and disagree with and why? Did any comments surprise you?

J: My own impacted me the most. I said some things that weren't really the best things to say. I agreed with all of the things said, except the ones that opposed my true beliefs. My own comments surprised me. Some words came out that weren't actually what I thought. It was a pretty big mistake, and I hope I don't really scare any[body] real bad.

What is most impressive to me is that these complex and profound transformations occurred in less than 24 hours. In his prewrite he proclaims that human research is "all bad"; within the same prewrite, he amended this to allow for research that is harmless or consensual. Implied here is a view that non-consensual, "harmless" research is appropriate, which would echo his earlier perspective (from September) about the case of Genie (Garmon 1994). Despite these qualifications, his preference remained for the preservation of human rights over the rights of science.

Soon after, his comments during the discussion became a source of classroom conflict, and eventually, inner turmoil for James himself. He became adamant about being able to take the lives of death-row inmates in the name of science, even without their consent. His tendency to prioritize the individual over science gave way to a strong prioritization of science, and many of his classmates became upset with his position. Later, James told me that the conflict he faced during class affected him a good deal. In fact, he went home and discussed what had occurred in class with his father. By the time he began to write his reflection for homework that evening, he was remorseful and had deviated from his earlier classroom statements. It is difficult to comprehend the metacognitive shift that occurred for him to judge his own position from earlier that day as the most surprising, and even disturbing. As with John looking back on his earlier learning theory writing, James seemed to be reflecting on his own views as though they had belonged to a complete stranger.

His final written reflection in June indicated that his views had stabilized somewhat and that his more egoistic comments had been ephemeral. In response to whether his views had changed over the course of the year, he wrote, "My position has changed. I'm not as prodeath as most of my classmates would put it. I don't say that we should test freely on jail inmates anymore. I just think that is unnecessary and that there are probably enough people that are willing to be tested on. I realized this and my position changed" (June 5, written assignment). In this final comment he had solidified his position that consent is essential even for death-row inmates, and he showed that he now was able to accurately recall the trajectory of his ethical views in a way that he could not from September through February.

On June 7 I had the chance to speak with James about his controversial views from March 8. He recalled, "I spoke what I thought and not what I believed" (June 7, interview). He indicated that he had needed a place to feel vague about his ideas and to work them out. By this last conversation he realized that his ideas were constantly changing and growing, and he believed that they would continue to change. However, he believed he would not budge in the future on one part of the issue—that human consent is always required, even for death-row inmates.

Abbey Tries On Controversial Stances

Abbey's case illustrates how adolescents in my research negotiated conflict for learning purposes. She began the year with a stance that clearly placed the rights of science before those of the individual. When she reacted to the case of Genie—the "closet child" studied by scientists—she wrote, "I think it was okay for scientists to take advantage of an opportunity that might never present itself again" (September 25, written). She believed that the researchers should have made their choices strictly according to what was best for the scientific method rather than what was best for the neglected child. Compared to her classmates, at this early point in the year, Abbey put forth a stance among the most strongly in favor of the interests of science.

This science-prioritized stance carried over to our first class discussion on human research, "If you can breed rats [for research] why don't you breed chimpanzees or humans or something?" (November 9, discussion). Her "lab-human" comment was the first in a series of stances by different students that became a focal point of class conflict on the issue of human research. This comment seemed to fall from the sky with no forethought and suggested either some students had never dealt with this ethical issue or perhaps they were just becoming cognitively capable of fully comprehending its implications.

As with the three other students who became the focus of classroom controversy, Abbey's moment espousing the controversial view brought up fairly immediate introspection and revision. By the end of the same conversation, she had backtracked and decided that we could not conduct lethal research on people who are already grown, but that research on already aborted fetuses would be acceptable. As with her lab-human comment above, Abbey's approach to human research was generally to ensure that animals had treatment equal to that of their human counterparts. This continued on December 8, when she presented another amended version of her human research stance: "I think that if people really want animal rights and things like that then they should treat animals and humans equally . . . by saying that we could take people who die if they are willing to once they are dead let people do autopsies on them to figure out things with their brain" (December 8, discussion).

Abbey's ethical trajectory could have been scripted by Lawrence Kohlberg himself: She was trying on somewhat controversial perspectives, meeting with social and personal disequilibrium, reflecting, and then taking on new cognitive perspectives to reconcile the previously contradicting views. She had moved from wanting to breed lab humans, to using aborted fetuses, to researching corpses of consenting individuals. All the while she empathized with the plight of lab animals, even equating the Nazi experiments on Jews to human treatment of animals.

On March 8, when James brought up his controversial belief that scientists should conduct research on unwilling death-row inmates, Abbey became his most heartfelt contender: "And just because you are in jail and did something really bad doesn't mean you don't have a say in what you should do. I think that everyone should have a say. They should be able to say that they want to be able to be used in this experiment or not" (March 8, discussion). From supporting the breeding of nonconsensual lab-humans to protecting the human rights of the worst criminals around, Abbey was teaching me about the unpredictable and complex world of adolescent ethical growth.

Henceforth, her prioritization of the individual over science seemed to persist, as she stuck to this perspective in all subsequent written reflections. For the remainder of the year she consistently insisted that informed consent is essential for all forms of research. Even her final June 5 reflection showed general consistency in her ethical stance, "The number one rule about research is that you need the subject's consent" (June 5, written).

Connecting Findings on Conflict to Previous Theory

For the adolescents in this research project, conflict with peers became essential to both the development of their views and awareness of this development. Students who experienced such conflict became more aware of their development than they had before, and their stances seemed to stabilize as a result. James is a case in point; his leftover frustration with getting ganged up on for his controversial view remained at the end of the year. However, he held strongly that the somewhat "negative" experience was an invaluable learning moment for him that was worth the pain. As he put it, "I took in what everybody said, it played around in my head, and slowly my ideas changed" (June 7, interview). In the end, the difficult experience lifted him to a more heartfelt and stable ethical view.

In the course of the year, a surprising four out of the six of my focus students took views that met with significant peer resistance during at least one class discussion. In some cases, the entire class seemed upset with one of the student's position and in other cases the controversial view met with noticeable and heated disagreement from a large set of students in class. I am not counting here classroom moments where only a few students disagreed with someone's view.

When asked to reflect on changes in their perspectives, all four of these students emphasized the moment their stance became the center of conflict in class discussion. In all four cases, students reported that the experience of classroom conflict initiated their gradual development of a more stable stance. Kohlberg's research supports my finding that conflict played an important role in their ethical development: "Presumably a sense of contradiction and discrepancy at one's own stage is necessary for reorganization at the next stage" (Kohlberg 1969, p. 403). Classrooms provide ideal contexts for students to come up against diverse and conflicting views from others in their peer group; or, as James put it, classrooms provide a context for students to say and receive feedback on what they think, and not only what they believe. Such conflict can only occur in a productive way, though, when teachers build in time and structures to facilitate this process.

Another important finding in relation to the issue of conflict was that those who had become the focus of conflict eventually backed away from their more controversial stances by amending them to incorporate opposing views. Kohlberg discusses this process of reconciliation that I observed with my students, "The more the individual is responsible for the decision of the group, and for his own actions in their consequences for the group, the more must he take the role of the others in it" (Kohlberg 1969, p. 399). According to Kohlberg, social conflict can be an effective catalyst for internal disequilibrium: When an individual's cognitive model comes into conflict with a social situation, the individual will develop a new cognitive approach that reconciles, or incorporates, that conflict. My research demonstrated that social conflict could be a wonderful developmental medium in the classroom setting as well. For the four students who had at some point become the center of classroom conflict, their ethical perspectives followed a common developmental trajectory:

- Student "tries on" perspective
- Student encounters social conflict
- Internal disequilibrium
- Reflection; mental "playback" of social conflict
- Amended view that reconciles original views with conflicting ones
- More stability of stance and awareness of changing nature of views

In my teaching practice I have discovered that conflict is a very important ingredient for the ethical development of adolescents. This project demonstrated to me that it is essential to provide a context for students to try on perspectives, to say what they think even if it is not well planned. Through this process, they are able to get feedback from those around them and to reconcile their views with the views of others. In this way, they use their classmates as teachers who help them move from an idea to a belief. If this project can contribute anything to the current dialogue about ethical and moral education, it is that ethical education needs to acknowledge and promote the expression of difference among student views. Models of ethical and moral development that are top-down and teach one system of belief prevent students from having this opportunity to open up the conversation to controversy.

Self-Awareness of Ethical Trajectories

At two times during the year I assessed whether or not students were aware of their own ethical development. The March 8 prewrite and the June 5 written reflection asked, "Have you held this position on human research since the beginning of the year or has your perspective changed? If it has changed, describe how your position has changed or grown. What led to your change of perspective?" On March 8, two students were accurate in recollecting their prior views, three were partially accurate, and one was completely inaccurate. On June 5, four students were accurate, and two were partially accurate. This group of six students seemed as a whole to get somewhat more accurate at recalling their earlier views and the trajectory of change their stances had taken. During the first half of the year, students were more likely to believe their ideas had not changed even where they had. By the end of the year, all six students had become more aware that their stances were dynamic rather than static.

Stabilization of Student Perspectives Over Time

When I began this project, I wanted to know if students would be able to solidify a particular stance, that is, that their stance would be consistent over time and across circumstances. By the end of the year, most students had established views that were more stable and more consistent than they had been at the beginning of the year. More specifically, they did not swing as often across classifications, and they echoed their prior views with more accuracy and confidence across all situations.

General Lessons for My Classroom

This project taught me that the development of ethical stances is a complex, as opposed to a linear, process. In general, students began the year with less stable ethical perspectives and less awareness of the content and dynamic nature of their stances. With ongoing reflective lessons built into my curricula, students moved toward more stable stances and better self-awareness of the content and trajectory of their views. At the end of the year, it pleased me to discover students who participated in my study were better aware of the changing nature of their ethical views than they had been in the first half of the year. They had become more willing to admit uncertainty in their positions and to discuss their perspectives as works in progress rather than finished products. This pleased me partly because it was a more accurate representation of their ethical development. And, secondly, it suggested that this cyclical reflective process of revisiting ethical positions might support ethical self-awareness.

By understanding their own process of ethical growth, I hope that students will be better positioned for future growth. I also hope that a deeper awareness of their own uncertainty may help students become more accepting of the views of others. By understanding their own views as works in progress, students may become less attached to their own views and more open to the possibility of change. With this, I imagine, they will approach the views of others with the same openness and patience. These are possible areas for future research.

More than anything else, this research project reaffirmed to me that schools must be explicit and intentional in providing an environment to support students in developing their ethical views. It required an entire year and many lessons for students to demonstrate a noticeable gain in the confidence and clarity of their views. A brief ethics unit could never have supported the growth I observed in this project; students need a lot of time to go through the process of trying on perspectives and reconciling their views with those around them. And even with all of the intentional reflection that I built into my program, a significant amount of private and public conflict remained unresolved.

From a teacher's perspective, the curricular battle is often between coverage and quality. The learning value of this reflective process has convinced me to make more room in my classroom agenda for ethical issues, even at the expense of covering fewer topics. When we do not do this as teachers, we risk graduating students who pull their ethical system out of the air. Furthermore, student engagement and participation were at their highest during these conversations about ethics. Each of the students I followed this year insisted that this was a valuable and relevant learning process, and five out of six told me they wished we had done even more with ethics. Ethical education seems to be on their minds and good for their minds.

[1] I realized when beginning to sort my data in this way that there were many aspects of my research that may not be compatible with Kohlberg's model, but I needed a place to begin. Kohlberg proposes six main stages of moral development—two in *preconventional,* two in *conventional,* and two in *postconventional.* Adolescents generally fall under only a couple of these six stages, so there would be very little variation in my sample. It is important also to note that I was tracking the views of a given student over the

course of only a year, while Kohlberg's work covered commonalities for large groups of people over a wide age range. While he looked across these stages, I most probably observed the development within a given stage. To further complicate the applications of his views, Kohlberg warns that there is often stage mixing for individuals within all of the stages.

Reflections

In Matt's study, the elements of questioning, collecting evidence, making sense of the evidence, and sharing take the form of formal research practices (see Table 1 in the Preface). The research process is in the foreground in this chapter, and it is clear that, as Matt plans his teaching, he is simultaneously planning his research. At the same time, his work is quite different from the work of a university researcher studying a teacher. The act of studying his own teaching informs his teaching on the deepest level. For example, Matt wrote, "One of the most significant data sets for my research came on March 8, when I decided to show my students footage of themselves from a videotaped conversation that had occurred about four months prior …. After reviewing this earlier conversation, I asked them to discuss together their reactions to watching it and to share any thoughts about the ethical issues involved." Matt is working from his guiding question, but he is planning and developing his way of finding the answer to the question as he interacts with his students from day to day.

In primary school, where one teacher teaches all the subjects, a teacher naturally sees the whole child in each student. In secondary school, it is natural for a science teacher to focus on science content, and it is difficult to find time to make the connections to other areas of life. Although not the stated objective of Matt's research, for many students, understanding the connection of science to other parts of their lives can inspire an interest in science that they may not otherwise discover.

References

Garmon, L. 1994. *The secret of the wild child* [Television series episode]. P. Apsell (Executive Producer), NOVA. Boston: WGBH.

Hayes, R. L. 1994. The legacy of Lawrence Kohlberg. *Journal of Counseling and Development,* 72(3): 261–268.

Kohlberg, L. 1969. Stage and sequence: The cognitive-developmental approach to socialization. In *Handbook of socialization theory and research,* ed., D. Goslin, pp. 347–480. New York: Rand McNally.

Kroger, J. 1996. *Identity and adolescence.* London: Routledge.

Palmer, P. J. 1999. Evoking the spirit. *Educational Leadership* 56(4): 6–11.

Walsh, C. 2000. The life and legacy of Lawrence Kohlberg. *Society* 37(2): 38–43.

Student Teaching as Collaboration

Claire Bove and Matthew Reider

Claire Bove has taught science for many years at an urban middle school in the San Francisco Bay area of California. As a Carnegie Scholar in the CASTL K12 program, she documented her teaching and students' learning on a website (http://feelingathome.org) for the use of teachers, prospective teachers, teacher educators, and others interested in teaching and learning. She currently meets regularly with several teachers who are studying their own practice. She also coordinates the Mills Scholars, a teacher inquiry group at Mills College.

Matthew Reider writes curriculum and teaches in a large urban high school near Oakland, California. He cowrote this chapter about his experiences as a student teacher in a middle school, also near Oakland, where he taught with Claire Bove. Recently they have worked on a number of different projects—both science related and not. One of these involved a student-produced video documentary about prison issues in California. Another focused on African American boys and the identity issues they faced in his classroom and in general.

For teachers who are trying to understand what their students think and how they feel, data can include notes found on the floor after class, the letters they as teachers write to their students, and the e-mails they send each other as they puzzle out the problems of teaching and learning. Claire and Matt use all of these data sources as they try to understand and respond to individual students' interests, strengths, experiences, and needs. In this story of their collaboration as cooperating teacher and student teacher, they document their efforts to support a classroom community in which cooperation, shared responsibility, and respect among students are built upon their own collaboration as teachers.

Introduction by Claire Bove

I am a teacher. In the morning I often find myself standing at the copy machine, watching the copies come out. I'm making copies for the day: 150 copies of each class handout. Before you read any further, take a stack of paper and count 150 sheets. Or pick up a book and pinch 150 pages between your figures. When I look at my stack of 150 sheets of paper, I see 150 young individuals. Each of my students will get one of these papers and make marks on it with a pen or a pencil or a Sharpie or a Magic Marker. Or a highlighter. Each student will inscribe a portion of his or her individuality on one sheet. After they do, I will stack the papers up again. The stack is no longer neat. Middle school students do not stack well.

The school where I teach is an urban middle school. It is economically, academically, linguistically, and ethnically diverse. There are 18 different languages spoken by families sending their children to the school. The ethnic breakdown is approximately 32% Latino, 28% African American, 30% white, and 10% Asian.

What follows is a story about middle-school students and their teachers. It happened when Matt was working with me as a student teacher and when I was in my sixth year of teaching. Like many stories, this one starts in the middle.

Part 1 by Claire Bove

Evidence of Learning

There is a moment right after class, an intensely quiet moment, when two dozen 12-year-olds have just left the room. A minute ago their energy was all around you; now, they're gone. It is not that they always run; it is not that they always shout when you set them free and they scatter in all directions. It is simply that, at all times, even in moments of quiet, their internal energy is turned up to its highest setting.

Matt and I looked at each other, breathed, and listened to the quiet. Usually, after they left, we had to laugh. Sometimes we laughed about a note found on the floor (See Figure 1). Sometimes about a conversation overheard on the way out. There is something poignant and just a little ridiculous about many conversations overheard in middle school. After we laughed, I asked Matt what he wanted to talk about that day. It was his class that had just left. The school is on block schedule, so one day I taught first period and he observed, the next day he taught second period and I observed.

Figure 1: Example of notes found on the floor

I keep a lot of these "found" notes because they seem to me like windows into the world where middle school students spend most of their time. Here's one:

"I'm sorry i didn't hear u and when garratt was poking me i thought he was doing that to bug me."
"It's OK"
"are we still friends ?
yes or no   circle one" [The "yes" was circled.]

Here's another:
   "Yes you did do something to me"
   "What did I do?"

To see scans of the actual notes, go to http:/mreider.com/notes.

Matt thought for a minute. He said that he didn't know if they were getting it. The concept we were attempting to teach was that flowers have strategies to get pollinators to come and pollinate them. They use color, scent, rewards, or mimicry, each species of flower using a system designed to attract a particular species of pollinator. It is a difficult concept: A flower, which has no brain, does something that looks very much like planning; over long periods of time, populations of individuals with the best strategies survive.

Did our seventh graders understand this? Did they understand anything about it? We spent much of our time writing engaging, well-planned, active lessons to keep our students interested. In the lesson Matt had just taught, students designed their own pollination strategies, then, two by two, they acted out pollination strategies in front of the class, with the aid of props which included plastic animals and a little basket of "pollen." During the class discussion, a few students raised their hands, a few were able to answer the questions. Others nodded their heads. But good instruction does not guarantee learning. It is difficult to tell whether students have learned what you have tried to teach.

I suggested that we look at what they were writing in their journals. Student writing sometimes tells you what students are getting from the lessons. It has to be a particular kind of writing, though. If the questions are too directed, if the answers are easy to guess from the context, then a student who is a good mind reader can tell what the teacher wants to hear, and the teacher may be fooled. A question that gets at student understanding and that invites a student to write enough so the teacher can tell something about what the student understands, that question is difficult to write.

Matt emptied the carton of spiral-bound notebooks onto one of the tables. The covers of the notebooks were all different colors. Some journals were neat, some were tattered, some were scribbled, and some were inscribed with care.

We started to flip open the journals and scan them for the question he had asked them to write about at the end of class: "What were all of the flowers trying to do with their different strategies?"

We spread the journals out with the question showing. The names were on the covers, so once we had the journals open we couldn't see whose was whose. Most students had copied the question at least. I knew many of the students by their handwriting, because I had taught them for a semester before Matt came to be their student teacher. He too knew their work without needing to see a name, because he had been teaching them since the beginning of February and we were now in May. But we were not trying to see who was saying what; we were reading for any evidence that the lessons, our engaging, well-planned, active lessons, were helping our students understand this concept.

After reading a few answers, I came to one that explained, in a most sophisticated and detailed way, exactly what we wanted students to understand about the pollination strategies of flowers. I read it out loud, in amazement and in awe.

I didn't recognize this handwriting. I turned to the front of the journal to find out whose it was—it belonged to a student named Jon. I had taught Jon in sixth grade and in the first semester of seventh. Jon often looked bored. He never raised his hand. But I would call on him if no one else volunteered for a hard question, because he never failed me and I didn't have to worry about embarrassing him by asking a question that was too hard for him. His journal was full of doodles: clever drawings of critters chasing critters, and aliens chasing aliens. Wonderful, imaginative drawings conveying motion and humor. His written science work, however, was minimal and sloppy. Jon was smart, quiet, thoughtful. He was the kind of kid I thought should like science. And for some reason, he didn't. He was the kind of student I thought I should be able to reach. And for some reason, I couldn't.

Now he was writing long, detailed answers. He was working carefully, thoughtfully, and his heart was in it. Even his handwriting had improved. I was astonished, and delighted, that Jon was realizing his potential. I asked Matt what had happened? What had he done to get Jon to blossom?

Does the Teacher Know Me?

Matt answered that he just kept telling Jon that he is smart. In different words, in different ways, he kept saying, over and over again "You are really smart." I asked him how he did that. What did he say? When did he say it? How did he say it? Matt told me that whenever Jon turned in a paper, he wrote a response to it. He complimented him on his answers, and he complimented him on his doodles. Matt said Jon knew he was smart, and it was easy to convince him that someone else thought so, too.

Every day Matt was taking home a pile of student papers and writing messages to each student. All Matt's students were getting specific and often lengthy comments from their teacher when they got their papers back.

Charisma Versus Practice

Even before this, I had seen that Matt was writing a lot on student papers and I had commented that I thought it was an excellent practice, but we hadn't really talked about it. Now we did. He told me he had started doing this with his high school class in the fall semester of his student teaching. He didn't always write just about their work. Sometimes he wrote about something that had happened in class, or gave them some encouragement to try harder. He wanted to make a personal connection with each of them and let them know he cared about each of them.

As Matt talked, I pictured students getting their notes. How nice it would be to get one of those notes from your teacher. And, knowing him as I did, I could see him writing them, could imagine him finding something that would speak to each of his students. But when I thought about doing it myself, I doubted that I would be able to do this. I felt very far removed from the world where they lived their real lives, the world they wrote about in the notes they left on my floor. What could I say that would be meaningful to them? Matt was closer to them in age and in experience. He was in his early 30s. I was 20 years older. I was learning a lot from him, but I didn't think I could learn this difficult lesson: how to reach my students.

He watched my face as he talked, and he could see something was bothering me. He said he knew he wouldn't be able to do it next year when he had five classes and 150 students. I had the feeling he was saying it partly as a look at his future, but also to let me know he knew I couldn't do it since I had so many more students.

His class was a good class for a student teacher. It was small, about 20 students. There were some students who had trouble learning. There were some whose behavior was not perfect. There were students he found particularly challenging and students he found particularly interesting, and often the challenging students and the interesting students were the same people. But for the most part the class was pretty manageable.

The class was responding to him, they liked him. I thought it was because he was young and cool and smart and fun, and, indeed, these characteristics did not hurt. Now I started to realize that what he was doing with these letters was central to the positive climate that was evident in his class.

When Matt said he wouldn't be able to write letters next year, that a teacher with a full schedule wouldn't be able to do it, I told him I wasn't sure that was true. I said that there are practices we do as student teachers that we do because they are so obviously right: calling *all* the parents, writing to each and every student. Everyone says you can't do these things once you start teaching full time. You hear it over and over again. But is it true?

Writing to each student is a powerful practice. Much more powerful than a lot of the things we spend our time on. What would happen, I asked, if we tried to imagine a way to do it when you are teaching full time? What if a full-time teacher tried it with just one class? What if I, for example, were to try it with my first-period class, the seventh-grade class he was watching me teach?

Learning to Teach and Learning to Be a Teacher

Matt's response surprised me. He said that he thought it was important for teachers not to keep taking on more and more work. That he didn't want me to find myself working harder than I was already because I was working with him. And that it was a luxury for him to teach only one class, to spend so much time thinking about these 20 kids, and to talk with me every day about the big and small issues that came up. But maybe he should be thinking about next year? Maybe he should be trying to figure out, to learn, the practical strategies a teacher has to have to be able to teach five classes?

While Matt felt it was a luxury for him to teach only one class, to me it was a luxury to have another teacher to teach with, to talk with every day. In the morning we took turns teaching and observing; in the afternoon he went to his college courses and I taught sixth-grade science. Each morning we talked after class, and usually we met on Friday afternoons to plan the next week. And we sent a lot of e-mail—lesson plans, handouts, and other thoughts.

In our conversations we talked about the specifics of teaching—how to sequence activities, what a particular student said and what he (or I) replied, and was that the best thing to say? We also talked about our thoughts, our philosophies of teaching. Here is a part of one e-mail Matt sent me in February, long before the day we looked at the journals together. He is writing about a lesson that didn't go well and about the conversation the two of us had had about it.

> *2/22/02*
> My class today: I just wanted to let you know that I DO appreciate your feedback—and that I seek negative criticism more than positive criticism because it helps me keep an eye on weak points. So keep that coming. It is a delicate dance—to listen and to give feedback. I think I can be a very critical person—and I am equally critical of myself. As the lesson unfolded today, I was very sensitive to what was not going well—could see this almost immediately. Yolanda was totally lost. Jasmine was totally lost. Some students started the opener by completing the homework they had not finished …

because I had commented in my notes to them that it was not finished. Lots of confusion. I am sure you noticed—but I actually sat with each kid and redefined the goals—in very simple terms. The fact that I had given them my written comments (2 sets of them) was like an assignment in itself (or 2 assignments—one for each comment sheet). So this pile of papers was very confusing, hypercomplex, and not developmentally appropriate.

An interesting social insight is what happened when you asked me "what went well—what did not go well?" I immediately thought of your asking me the same question a week ago—and at that time I had answered you with a lot of negative comments (regarding the digestive theater lesson). Last week you thought I was beating myself up too much. So this week I tried to tone that down a bit. I can beat myself up pretty easily ... sometimes it is deserved. So today—maybe I should have verbalized all of the GUILT I had about the lesson—but instead I focused on the positive ... mostly because of our conversation a week before and also due to my awareness that I am not always on the mark when I attack myself (or others). So if you saw my eyes glaze over when you reviewed the foibles of the lesson—it may have been that part of me wishing that I had told you what I really saw—what I really thought.

Teaching with another teacher watching, whether you are the student teacher or the cooperating teacher, makes you feel very vulnerable. When you screw up, as often happens in the unpredictable world of teaching, you know—or imagine—that the other teacher can see what you did wrong. You feel exposed: It's almost like being naked. When I was teaching, I tried to accept this vulnerability, not to hide it. In response to what Matt wrote, I told him some of my doubts about my own teaching. Even at this early point in our work together, I was aware of his ability to talk to students in a way that engaged them and my own inability to do that. This is part of the answer I wrote him:

> *2/23/02*
> Matt, the kind of information you are giving me will, I hope, I think, make our work productive. "It is a delicate dance—to listen and give feedback." This is an accurate and beautiful way to say it. My goal in coaching you is to help you achieve as much growth as possible in your teaching during this short time—probably the only time you will have someone observing you every day with the purpose of working on your teaching. I don't think it is a good idea, usually, to compare teachers to each other (just because we are all here for the kids, and we are all trying for our personal best, and there is way too much competition between people in general), but I will do it a little bit to give some context to where I am as a coach. I have worked

with four other new teachers (student teachers and first year teachers) ... I would say you are more like a good second-year teacher than a student teacher. And in some areas your development is beyond mine—I would not have been able to do the digestion drama lesson, or the mountaineering talk, the way you did. And not because I don't climb mountains—the idea of being able to tell about yourself in a way that engages students—I am not there yet. And the digestion lesson—I would have to think about it a lot, and have a couple of unsuccessful experiences teaching it before it was as good as yours was.

Deciding to Write the Letters

The arguments against my trying Matt's letter-writing practice were strong. I would have to find the time somewhere in my life. But where? My life, like that of most teachers, was like a land that had been frequently raided and robbed by time thieves. Time: the patch that once was "reading" was gone. "Exercise," gone. "Seeing friends," gone. What was left? There was "lesson planning" and "experiment setup" and "grading" and "sleep." Sleep wasn't all gone, but every New Year's resolutions list I had written in the last six years began: Get more sleep. Furthermore, the end of the year is a strange time to start something.

In spite of the arguments against the letter writing, the evidence of potential benefits was too strong to ignore. There was the positive climate in Matt's class, which was probably a result of the letters, and the transformation in the work of one student, which was clearly and directly a result of this practice. I decided to try it with my first period seventh-grade class. The day we read Jon's journal was about four weeks before the end of the semester, so I didn't have much time.

Seeing a Student Through His Story

After the pollination lesson we moved on to human reproduction. One of the first assignments was to "tell a story about a baby you know: It could be you, or it could be a little brother or sister, a neighbor or a cousin." I used these stories and student journal writing as a basis for my letters to the students. One of my students, Dante, had done little work all year. His story about the baby was not long, but it was longer than usual. It was about his two-year-old cousin. She fell off the bed, she cried, and then she stopped crying and laughed. She was naughty and always looking for trouble. It was short, and it conveyed deep feeling. I spent a long time puzzling over the story, trying to figure it out. Why was he writing about her? What had happened that he hadn't included in the story? What was Dante's view of himself, and could I discover it through this story? Who is he? As I tried to write this letter, I thought more about Dante than

I had all year. I returned the story to him, and I don't have a copy of it. But here is the letter I wrote to him:

5/26/02
Dear Dante,

I was reading your journal, and I read the one on Friday, May 10, where you said humans and plants are similar because they both have little babies, but they are different because in plants there is no stomach for them to come out of. That is an important difference, and I don't think anyone else thought of it.

I like your story about your baby cousin. I'm curious to know, when she fell off the bed, and she started to cry, but then she started to laugh, what made her laugh? Are you the one who got her to laugh?

It is cool that she has so much spirit. Maybe she takes after you.

I also like how you wrote more than usual. Do you think that having a homework assignment where you can tell a story makes it easier for you to write more?

Sincerely,

Ms. Bove

Up to this point in the year, Dante's behavior had sometimes been good and sometimes not so good. A short time before this exchange of writing, I had moved his seat from the back of the class to the front, and he was doing a little better at paying attention sitting right in front of me than he had when he was in the back. After he got this short letter from me, his behavior changed dramatically. Not only did he behave well, he started telling other people to behave. He became my ally. And then one day I leaned my hand on his desk, palm down, and he put his thumb and first finger around my wrist, like a bracelet. I felt that he was saying to me, "I know you like me."

No other student responded to one of these letters quite as strongly as Dante. But there was something in the way the students looked at me, spoke to me, that was subtly different. Their eyes met mine more often. They smiled more.

The thing that surprised me most, however, was not the response of the students to me, but my own response to them. Sitting by myself at home on Saturday, reading a story by a student, trying to see who that young person is, getting enough of a picture of him or her to write a letter, that was what changed me. Even those students who did not respond in any obvious way looked different to me because I had thought about them and tried to imagine how they thought about themselves.

Student Achievement

The next fall, Dante was in the eighth grade, and I saw him one day helping his PE teacher carry equipment out to the field. He smiled at me and put down what he was carrying. He came up to me and gave me a hug. It made me feel wonderful to know he liked me. But what is more important, I think, is that he felt that kind of warmth toward an adult, a teacher, someone whose job it is to educate him and help him succeed in the world of school. I don't know if that connection made any difference to his learning. With Jon, the personal connection Matt made with him clearly made a difference in his academic performance. With Dante, it was the end of the year and I didn't know.

Politicians, policy makers, and administrators keep telling teachers that our practice must be driven by the achievement data, that our job is to close the achievement gap. But learning must precede achievement, and learning is complicated. Forming a bond with another human being, with a teacher, is a risk for a young person: a risk that can lead to the discovery that connection is meaningful and that learning is meaningful. It is most important, and riskiest, for African American students and Latino students, who are marginalized by the educational system and who are at the bottom of the achievement gap. It can take a long time to convince a student like Dante that I want to know who he is, that I like him, that I believe in him. There is a value in making a connection with another person, a value independent of and more important than its effect on achievement. Ultimately a bond of this kind can change both the student and the teacher, the way it did for Dante and me.

Student Teachers

From that time to this, I have written many more letters, and I have worked on a series of other strategies to help me learn about my students, to like them, to understand them a little, to value them as individuals, and to communicate my feelings to them, to open myself up to them. It is the most interesting and the most powerful part of my practice. My students now come in each day with minds that are a little more receptive than in the past. More of what I say to them goes inside; less is deflected, resisted, rejected. I would not have come here on my own. The work Matt and I did together brought me here.

The student teachers I have worked with—three at this writing—have all been smart. And highly motivated. They think about teaching all the time. In their college courses, they are learning, discussing, reading, and arguing about teaching. When they come to me to practice, I listen to them, and I try to figure out what issues they find the most interesting, the most compelling in their teaching. And these have turned out to be the ones I care about: reaching students, engaging them, turning them on to learning. Together we work on those issues. I lend them some of my experience, they lend me some of their passion for teaching. I learn from them, and they learn, too. Learning is often about making a connection with another person. This is as true for teachers as it is for students.

Part 2 by Matt Reider
Fall Assignment

My year as a student teacher began at a convenience store a hundred yards from the gates of the college where I had just enrolled. Grabbing some food before my first class started, I wandered toward the cashier. He looked anxious. As he rang me up he told me the store had been robbed that morning. Handing me my change, he asked what I did for a living

"I am a teacher," I said, knowing that this was not technically true. I was not even a *student* teacher yet. But it seemed simpler than the full explanation. "Teaching is a tough job," the man replied. I wondered if the anxiety I saw in his face was similar to what he saw in mine.

My fall assignment was to work with a teacher named Doug who taught marine biology at a large urban high school. I would observe his first-period class and teach his second. On the first day of school I watched Doug squeeze his class into randomly assigned seats and take roll. Some of the boys were more than six feet tall, and the desks barely held them. I felt nauseous as the bell rang and Doug's students pulled their baggy jeans up over their hips to exit the classroom. The next set of teenagers trickled in and got situated. "I am your teacher, Mr. Reider," I said. My voice was unsure but determined.

My nausea eased as I learned my students' stories. Isaac was a 16-year-old who lived near the beach with his father. Tien was a tiny girl who wore her JROTC military uniform every day. She had a smile that could solve armed conflict. Chris sat in the hallway before class hoping for the chance to set up microscopes or plankton nets. By late September the classroom seemed a friendlier place. Sometimes learning science was exciting. Other days it was boring, but we were usually in it together.

Yet some students seemed neither friendly nor interested in science. Two boys in particular, Bryan and Malcolm, were creating an *F* column straight down my grade book. Both slumped in their seats, never making eye contact, shrouding their heads in huge oversized jackets as if they wanted to be invisible. Sitting down to talk with them it was hard to sense their pulse. I did not know how to reach them.

On September 11, the day the World Trade Center collapsed, I faced my students and tried to comfort them. One of my students wondered if I was worried about my friends in New York. All of them knew I was from the East Coast and they were as concerned about my mental health as I was about theirs. I admitted that I was sad and that I had some friends who worked near Wall Street. All of us were confused and emotional as we tried to make sense of the world that day. As we shared our feelings, I was surprised that both Malcolm and Bryan were part of the discussion. As I talked about my own sadness, Bryan listened intently. He appeared to have tears in his eyes.

Bryan's tears gave me hope, something all of us needed to feel during that time. He also allowed me to see him as a vulnerable young man—much more than the defiant, scary teen who never did his homework. I was determined to connect with both Bryan and Malcolm. Since talking was difficult, I wrote letters instead.

My first letter was to Malcolm. I wrote about a time when I smelled his fingers and asked whether or not he had been smoking pot. I may have been gentler about the accusation than he was used to; he let me sniff without a fuss. His fingers smelled like breakfast, so I apologized and walked away. Looking back at me, Malcolm asked, "Mr. Reider, are you a psychologist or something?" I broke out laughing. Toward the middle of the letter, I wrote about my love for science and tried to make a connection for him: "The cartoons in your notebook remind me of animals somewhere in an imaginary branch of the evolutionary tree." I wrote about how hard it was for me when he said the subject matter was stupid or silly. I tried to explain that this was like telling him that basketball or hip-hop was a waste of time—things he loved and would defend. I cared about the things that interested him, and at the end I told him I cared about him.

My next letter was to Bryan. I congratulated him for handing in some homework and let him know that his writing was fun for me to read. I mentioned my love for science again and how wonderful it was to live near the water and see so much wildlife.

After receiving my letters, Bryan started making eye contact with me during class. Malcolm also cheered up. He even hugged me the day of his final exam, but his performance in class did not improve. Bryan's grades, on the other hand, ambled upwards. His journal, virtually empty during the first half of the semester, was now a mixture of science work and sarcasm. It was a big improvement. Doug took over my class when I was reassigned to Claire's school in the spring. "Bryan sends his regards," he told me in March. He was earning a B.

I wrote letters to all of my students that semester. Through this experience I came to believe that writing letters to students can be more effective than talking. There was no act they had to put on as they read my notes. They did not have a chance to say things like "yeah, whatever," as they might during a conversation. They could read something personal, in private, and, I hope, feel special that I spent time thinking about them. Recently, I went to a neighborhood restaurant and was seated by a host who recognized me as "Mr. Reider." She quoted the letter I had written to her two years before.

Spring Assignment

The middle school where Claire worked was a 10-minute drive away. A group of boys were playing basketball in the school playground when I arrived—tall boys with colorful faces blocking shots and running back and forth in pursuit of a dark orange ball. I wondered which ones would be in my class. The nausea returned.

This first meeting with Claire occurred a week before she introduced me to my students. I told her about my decision to leave the high-tech industry and become a teacher. I wanted to find more meaning than the corporate world seemed to offer. I did not talk about the queasiness I felt watching the boys playing basketball outside. My words were like sheets of plastic—carefully placed over the fear and uncertainty beneath.

Before I took responsibility for teaching her second-period class, I observed Claire in action. I started to realize how much there was to learn. She had a calendar for each student to keep track of homework and a system to inform parents of missing assignments. She used an overhead projector instead of a chalkboard so she could face the class at all times. When the class was off-task she raised her hand to indicate that things were too noisy or she thanked certain students for their behavior until the idea caught on. She rang a xylophone like chimes to calm them and refocus their attention. To the side of the class, a student stood up on cue and adjusted a sign indicating different "modes." There were quiet modes when students were silent and other modes where talking or moving around was acceptable. None of these routines felt familiar to me.

Between classes, during 10-minute breaks, hundreds of students ran around an open patio making accusations about romance and stolen teddy bears. This was middle school. In Claire's class, however, there was mostly patience and kindness. When Justin, a disruptive and angry 12-year-old, threw erasers at human targets, Claire made him sit after class to think silently by himself. Watching him, I could tell that Justin actually felt bad. I think he felt that he had let her down. There was a special quality to Claire's relationship with her students. You could describe it only as love.

In Doug's class, I wrote personal letters to counterbalance the impersonal harshness of a crowded school. Writing letters felt natural to me, but Claire was also reaching students through her teaching methods, something I needed help to understand. Claire was doing the same. She was giving her students the feeling that they were human beings, not marks in a grade book.

I taught middle school science for five months as Claire observed me from the corner of the room. As I guided the class through activities, Claire scribbled notes. She rarely wrote her opinions. There was never bad nor good. She only wrote what the students did and said and what I did and said. Our postclass dialogues would start with my account of how things went and what I wanted to talk about. She would give me her observations as well, but she was mindful about keeping the conversation positive. Through these unthreatening exchanges my identity as a teacher began to solidify.

To teach individual students, we tried to figure out what was going on inside of them. One student we talked about was Aiesha, a stubborn 12-year-old who rarely handed in her homework. Our class was studying the water cycle, how molecules of water evaporate into the air, condense as clouds, and fall back again as rain. Aiesha would not touch her pencil. She told me that she did not want to do her work because it was too hard and she was stupid.

After a few more discussions with Claire, I called on Aiesha to answer a question about how water molecules condense to form clouds. It was a big concept, but we had talked about it often enough that I felt she could handle it. Her response was wonderful and accurate. I took a step back and shouted, "Wow, Aiesha, that's right! You know what? You are really SMART!" The look on her face made me float.

Aiesha needed affirmations about her intelligence. It was also important for her to understand that being smart did not mean having the right answer. Progress, especially in scientific research, is made by trial and error. But a lesson that pushes some students toward failure will eventually convince students like Aiesha that they are stupid. Claire helped me to understand that a good lesson can promote a feeling of success in every student, no matter what their level. She also challenged me to design lessons where confidence building was part of the learning process itself. I struggled to figure this out.

Together, we designed a lesson with confidence in mind. The students used magic markers to draw pictures of the water cycle—colorful scenes of sunlight, rain, trees, and rivers. No words were allowed on the posters, and each picture was unique, individual. When the pictures were complete, they affixed sticky notes to their posters and wrote the definitions of *condensation, precipitation, runoff,* and *evaporation.* They took the posters home to study them. When it came time to assess their understanding, we collected the sticky notes and they wrote the definitions once again, silently, for a grade.

Aiesha was using her pencil, so we took that as a sign that she did not feel stupid but instead confident enough to take the risk of trying. The lesson was effective because her creativity was the context for the science she was learning. Aiesha's poster was colorful and fun, something she was proud of, and she managed to label almost all of the steps. Her definitions showed that she got it. In the margin, I wrote "Aiesha, remember that day you said you weren't smart? Anyone who knows how condensation works is *definitely* smart!"

I taught Aiesha the following year before the school administration discovered that she lived in another district. One day her mother appeared, gathered Aeisha's things and closed the door behind them. I never saw Aeisha again.

Unlike Aiesha, Jon was self-confident but messy. He was uncomfortable in his own skin. His body was changing—he had pimples, a budding mustache, and a deepening but somehow squeaky voice. Like the rest of his body, his brain was in hormonal transition too, as evidenced by the ink blotches, scribbles, cartoons, and half-ripped pages in his journal.

Grading his journal was more of an amusement than an obligation. His cartoon characters had gotten themselves into all sorts of horrible situations. Some had been run over by cars, others were being skewered with swords. But it was Jon's writing that fascinated me most. In many of his entries he used a science concept as the premise for a good joke. He would start a paragraph about the water cycle with something like, "Disdain for rain? Proud of clouds? Condensation fixation? Have I got a cycle for you!"

In his journal, I wrote that I loved his drawings but that he had to make them smaller and not draw so much during class. The ink blotches had to go—it was a waste of paper. The writing was amazing. "Jon, I think someday you could be a writer." I asked if he could write the same way while showing me a little more about what he was learning. Jon knew that this was an honest request, because I was really curious about what he was thinking. By midterm his journal was still fun to read, but now he was writing primarily about science.

The next year, as a full-time teacher at the same middle school, I had five classes and 150 eighth-grade students. Finding time to meet with Claire was challenging, but we did it. Working with Claire as a student and a colleague, I discovered why collaboration is so important, for teachers and students alike. As with the science itself, our progress as science teachers happened because we asked questions and experimented. Doing this alone, we would have been limited to our individual experiences. But by blending our world views, we emerged with something new.

Reflections

The elements of teacher research in the previous chapter were all in the form of formal research practices. In this chapter, all the elements are present, but they are, for the most part, embedded in normal teaching practices, and intentional research practices (see Table 1 of the Preface). Claire and Matt were not conducting a study and did not think of themselves at the time as doing teacher research. But the act of sharing brought each of the elements forward as they looked at their teaching practices. Matt was in a rigorous preservice program, Claire was a member of a highly collaborative science department, and, when in their conversations, questions emerged about student learning, they naturally turned to the evidence that they gathered daily in the classroom: journals, student work, and student utterances. Their sense making around student learning drew them to examine new evidence: notes to students, notes from students, observations of student behavior, and journal entries. Their awareness of the relevance of all the evidence around them, including the unconventional evidence of notes picked up off the floor, reveals a research perspective in their orientation to teaching. When they came to write this description, the evidence they had collected to inform their teaching allowed them to write an evidence-based narrative of their experience to share with other teachers.

Reflections on Researching While Teaching

Researching while teaching occurs naturally for teachers who notice and wonder about aspects of their students' learning. However, the realities of schools present challenges for systematic inquiry. This set of case studies considers ways that individuals and groups of teachers can make progress in the face of such challenges. Dorothy Simpson shares her study of collaborative conversations and proposes that such ongoing intentional reflections are a practical form of teacher research. Teaching both children and prospective teachers, Christopher Horne reflects upon his experiences in giving—and finding—space as a teacher and researcher. Sometimes teachers assist one another in improving upon their teaching practices through coaching and participating in a teacher study group. Diantha Lay describes teacher study groups that formed within her school with support from her county for this form of professional development. A group of four teachers from different schools, Judy Fix, Norma Fletcher, Dianne Johnson, and Janet Siulc, discuss their students' responses to inquiry and their finding that listening closely to students has become an increasingly important aspect of their teaching practices. Deborah Roberts describes a physics experience she had as an undergraduate student that was so powerful she could not help but share it with students from first to eighth grade as well as teacher colleagues. In this chapter, she reflects upon ways in which using motion detectors to foster inquiry can get students and teachers to be movers and shakers in their own right. In the final chapter, Emily van Zee considers ways in which she fosters collaborative inquiries into science learning and teaching in teaching courses and in sponsoring teacher inquiry groups.

Chapter 9

Collaborative Conversations and Intentional Reflections on Teaching and Learning Physics

Dorothy Simpson

Dorothy Simpson taught mathematics for 15 years before she started teaching physics at Mercer Island High School near Seattle. Examples of her conversations with students can be seen in the "Can We Believe Our Eyes" segment of the Private Universe Project video "Minds of Our Own" produced by the Harvard-Smithsonian Center for Astrophysics (www.learner.org/resources/series28.html) and in "Why Don't You Tell Me the Answer" video about inquiry teaching produced by Northwest Regional Educational Laboratory (www.nwrel.org/msec/science_ing/resources.html). Now retired, she is serving as a volunteer at a local elementary school with special interest in providing support for the science units used there. In this chapter, she notes that it is very difficult, if not impossible, for classroom teachers to do the kind of research university people do. Teachers do not have enough time or resources for an in-depth research project. There is no one to hold a video camera; there is no time to transcribe conversations with students. What Dorothy proposes is that classroom teachers think of research as intentional reflection on their own work. Intentional reflection means reflection during time set aside for that purpose when teachers can make notes or write in a journal. One outcome of her intentional reflections was an article published in the November 1997 issue of The Science Teacher, reprinted here, about the collaborative conversations that she facilitated in her high school physics classroom.

Collaborative Conversations: Engaging Students in Dialogues

Many years ago the idea of discussing concepts with students in a mathematics context was presented at a workshop I attended. Since then I have continually tried to improve upon the process of letting my physics students develop their own ideas to reach a logical conclusion.

I believe this is a great method for helping students talk about their ideas, develop them logically, and reach some understanding of the process of science and the way real scientists work. These classroom discussions certainly fit the National Science Education Standard B requirements for focusing and supporting inquiries, orchestrating discourse, challenging students, and encouraging and modeling skills of scientific inquiry (NRC 1996, p. 32).

The teacher's role in orchestrating discourse, according to the National Science Education Standards, "is to listen, encourage broad participation, and judge how to guide discussion—determining ideas to follow, ideas to question, information to provide, and connections to make" (p. 36).

Such discourse is very different from a lecture in which a teacher explains physics principles and demonstrates ways to solve physics problems. Such discourse also differs from a recitation in which a teacher asks students to explain physics principles and demonstrate ways to solve physics problems. Such discourse involves reflection, not only on what one knows but also on how one knows something and why one believes that to be the case (Minstrell 1989; van Zee and Minstrell 1997).

Ideas for Dialogue

The following presents my strategies for encouraging dialogue with students, from eliciting preconceptions to bringing closure to a unit. These strategies might provide a point of departure for teachers embarking on this approach for the first time or some insights for teachers more experienced with this approach to teaching.

The structure of a unit is shown in Figure 1 (p. 90). For students to develop "big ideas" through dialogue, they need to start with a familiar situation to which they can relate. The situation should take the form of a preinstructional exploration activity that encourages students to explore relevant physics ideas.

A dialogue about the exploration activity encourages further thought and curiosity about the physics involved. After this dialogue, students work on developing the concepts through demonstrations and activities in a logical sequence. Small-group discussions provide the basis for class development of the big ideas related to the unit. The small groups present their ideas to the rest of the class, and then there is a dialogue about the development activities in which students introduce evidence to support or refute each idea. The class narrows the list as the students reach logical conclusions about each idea.

The teacher-mediated discussions lead to closure as the students use logical reasoning about the observations to establish inferences that physicists would consider acceptable. During discussions I use the strategies presented in Figure 2 (p. 90). I specifically discuss with students my expectation that they will

Figure 1: Structure of a unit

Preinstruction (exploration) activity
- Present situation from which to elicit student preconceptions

Dialogue about exploration
- Open out dialogue—many possibilities
- Develop hypothesis

Development activities
- Look for questions about situation
- Look for inferences to support observations

Dialogue about development activities
- Start closing
- Reexamine preinstruction ideas
- Analyze for logic, consistency, validity, and reasonableness

Dialogue for closure
- Foster logical evolution of ideas toward thinking of physicist

Figure 2: Strategies for teachers during a dialogue

- Are you inviting all students to speak without judging their comments?
- When opening a discussion, are you refraining from commenting on student ideas and remaining noncommittal regarding your own ideas?
- Have you listed ideas on a board or overhead projector before discussion?
- Do you ask for supporting evidence for each comment after all are elicited?
- Do you ask questions to help the student construct a logical conclusion?
- Do you refrain from "telling" the student the pieces he or she is struggling to construct?
- Do you paraphrase each comment?
- Do you validate each speaker with an acknowledging comment?
- Do you provide wait time after a question, before allowing comments?
- Do you ask for counterarguments for each idea after all ideas are elicited?
- Do you ask questions that direct a student's thinking to a conclusion showing the fallacy of the argument?

improve or develop the skill of asking good questions by considering the implications of the points listed in Figure 3 (p. 91).

Figure 3: Student strategies during a dialogue

Active listening
- Do you listen carefully to what the speaker is saying?
- Do you listen from the point of view of the speaker?
- Do you actively consider the ideas presented?
- Do you try to find a pattern in the observations and ideas of other students?
- Do you mentally paraphrase what the speaker said?
- Do you think of what questions you could ask the speaker to clarify?
- Do you think about the observations and look for missing pieces?

Contributing
- Do you indicate your desire to speak without interrupting the speaker?
- Do you make comments that further the discussion about the ideas just presented?
- Do you ask questions about what the speaker said?
- Do you ask for clarification of what the speaker said?
- Do you challenge what the speaker said, based on your evidence?
- Do you refer to the ideas presented rather than to the person who introduced the ideas?
- Do you try to present arguments and counterarguments to the ideas presented?

Preinstructional Exploration Activity

Preinstructional activities create a context for student thinking by presenting some familiar situations related to the concepts in the unit. A possible exploration activity for a unit about forces might be students drawing force vectors on a diagram of the motion of a tossed ball. Discussion of the ball's motion provides a natural motivation for students to attempt to come to consensus about the forces in the situation.

I open the dialogue about the exploration activity with a discussion about any preconceived notions of the physics concepts involved. I then place ideas on the board or overhead projector for students to consider and I invite students to give reasons from real-life observations about why they think as they do. An example of a student idea might be that there needs to be a force on the ball in the direction of motion (McDermott 1984); in this case, students often propose that such a force would be provided by the hand. Our goal is to help students apply their understanding that hands cannot exert a force if they are not touching an object (other than gravitational force).

Possible questions for the dialogue about the exploration activity include:
- What do you think might happen?
- What experiences have you had to support your idea?
- Does that always happen?
- What might be some reasons why _____ would not happen?

Teacher Research

- What other possibilities might you suggest?
- Who has a different idea about what might be happening?

As students discuss their ideas, they try to create logical arguments and develop tentative hypotheses. Helping students focus on what they believe stimulates their thinking and gives them a starting point from which to compare observations and final inferences. During this discussion, students consider evidence for counterarguments. They also revisit concepts such as forces touching and forces at a distance.

Development Activities

Development activities engage students in examining their ideas further with demonstrations or hands-on experiments. Students record and discuss observations within lab groups. During these activities they ask questions about what is happening and continue to consider their predictions. They might think of related situations and form additional "What if ..." questions and then develop their own experiments to test their hypotheses. During this phase of the unit, students develop ideas to present as suggested big ideas from their group.

During the dialogue about the development activities, students elaborate and develop their ideas by reviewing the observations from the development activities. It is important that the observations be accurate enough that students can make valid deductions about the concepts. For example, students can move dynamics carts on a frictionless track and observe that they tend to continue at a constant velocity. At least one student will remember Newton's law of inertia and apply it to this situation, which is similar to that in which a ball is thrown horizontally. This result is in contrast to the students' initial hypothesis. By discussing the ideas from all lab groups, more information is presented for finding patterns.

In a dialogue about the remembered ideas and the pattern that is formed, students develop their ideas and follow their reasoning to a logical inference. This discussion helps students move from observations to inferences, using logical arguments to reach logical conclusions. They consider how valid their inferences are and the reasonableness of their conclusions. The comparison of the predictions from the exploration activity with the experimental observations is a critical part of the process of leading students to understand the concepts. The contrast between what students expect and what they observe or conclude is often an "aha!" experience that helps them to mesh their original ideas with the logic of the conclusions.

Possible questions for dialogue about the development activity include:
- What is your evidence for that idea?
- What was your observation?
- What might you infer from that observation?

Dialogue for Closure

I move toward closure by asking a variety of checking questions and carefully observing students' nonverbal expressions. Many ideas have been tossed about, and some students may have become confused with all the possibilities. Some students may have tuned out from active thinking about the inferences. Those students need to be pulled back into focus.

As the dialogue about the observations and inferences reaches a conclusion, it is important for the teacher to ask if the students agree about the conclusion. The agreed-upon conclusion needs to be repeated several times in several ways so all students understand it and can mentally agree with it. If any students still have questions, it might be necessary to reopen the discussion with some pertinent points of the logical sequence from observation to big idea to help the doubting students follow the logic. It is critical at closure that the conclusions on which the students agree also conform to good scientific thought.

General Comments About Questions

When teachers start using this process to help students think critically about the predictions, observations, and inferences, the dialogues usually tend to be dominated by teacher questions with student responses. As students become accustomed to the process and as they practice logical thinking and mental debate of the ideas, they will start asking questions. The student questions need to be answered with a teacher question that helps them move along in the logical reasoning.

As the process evolves, other students will become involved, and some of the best reasoning dialogues will involve students only, bypassing the teacher entirely. This is a very valuable learning situation in which students talk and reason with each other. They are thinking and have matured in their ability to reason logically so they can move to conclusions without the crutch that the teacher questions provide.

To negotiate a dialogue of logical thinking leading to physics' big ideas, the teacher needs to use a variety of techniques. Guiding the discussion requires a great deal of focus on listening and processing the comments. Before the dialogue can occur, the teacher must create a safe atmosphere so each student feels free to take a risk and make a statement without fear that it might be wrong. The teacher should remind students that there are no right or wrong statements in these dialogues.

The teacher must make choices about the direction of the dialogue. Is this a comment that requires more probing? Is this a comment that might lead the class astray or add confusion? What question will help direct the conversation back to the big idea or help a student redirect his or her thinking? Is this a dialogue to open up the student ideas, a dialogue to consider observations and inferences, or a dialogue for closure, culminating with the big ideas? Negotiating dialogues in this way requires much work by the teacher, who strives to maintain the direction of the discussion, but the payoff is understanding gained by students.

Intentional Reflection on the Teaching and Learning of Physics Through Inquiry

When we as teachers think of research, the term brings thoughts of university people coming to the classroom, giving activities or tests to students they don't know, and going away to write about it. Sometimes the results are relayed back to the teacher, and sometimes they aren't. Rarely do the results provide constructive means to improve the learning or teaching in that classroom.

It is very difficult, if not impossible, for K–12 classroom teachers to do the kind of research university people do. Teachers do not have enough time or resources for an in-depth research project. There is no one to hold a video camera and no time to transcribe conversations with students. Teachers have a huge load in their assignment of knowing content, using best teaching practices, helping less able students, supporting gifted students, working with disruptive students, assessing, and maintaining the paper trail. Would the effort expended to intentionally reflect on one's own practices assist in making the job manageable while improving the quality of the teaching?

What I propose would be for classroom teachers to think of research as *intentional reflection* on their own work. Teachers are all reflective about their own practices, although most are not systematically reflective. Intentional reflection means reflection during time set aside for that purpose and making notes or writing in a journal. These reflections provide a basis for considering a next step or what might have been done better. The ability to remember issues or ideas from a class increases with practice, and the skill of reflecting intentionally increases at the same time. What is necessary for teachers to improve upon their teaching practices? How high a priority is it for teachers to take the time to be intentionally reflective? How much does the act of writing thoughts about a lesson contribute to the improvement of teaching and learning for that teacher and the students? Does the process of writing reflections increase the thoughtfulness about the teaching practices? Does the act of writing down reflections lead to more reflections? Could it lead to ideas about better ways of presenting the material or additional activities to help clarify the big idea for better understanding by students?

Learning to Be Intentionally Reflective

My experience as a physics teacher leads me to believe that my quality of instruction and my success in gaining student understanding increased dramatically when I started using written reflections about my teaching practices. I had the privilege and luxury of having two mentor teachers encouraging my intentional reflections about my teaching as I made the transition from an experienced math teacher to a novice physics teacher. James Minstrell, the high school physics teacher at my school, had invited me to join his project to consider how best to teach physics for understanding at the high school level. The James S. McDonnell Foundation had provided funding so that he could spend part of the school day researching as well as teaching. I taught several of his classes with his coaching. As I was starting to share the physics duties with Dr. Minstrell, he suggested I keep a journal. I was frequently able to sort out my own ideas and dilemmas by writing my thoughts. From this first writing I was able to consider how my classroom practices encouraged all students—those with incredible ability in physics, those who struggled with logical thinking and big ideas, and all those in between. I reflected on what made my classroom a safe place for students and on how less-assertive girls and boys could be comfortable and enjoy the physics class. I reflected on the techniques I used for classroom discussions, trying to remember what was said and what better questions I could have asked to improve students'understanding. A paper on encouraging girls in physics evolved from these reflections (Simpson 1992).

As part of this project, Emily van Zee, a postdoctoral researcher from the University of Washington, videotaped my classes and helped me analyze my questions. As this process continued over a period of weeks, I became more analytical and careful about the questions I asked so that I could lead a class discussion from observation to a logically thought-out conclusion. As I was modeling the process of logical thinking, I was becoming much more adept at focusing on the conversation and providing questions that would either open the conversation or start the closure process, depending on where the student understanding seemed to be (Simpson 1997).

Sage Upon the Stage? Or, Is There a Better Way?

Teaching through inquiry is quite time consuming compared to teaching a traditional lecture course. My students have occasionally requested that I tell them what I want them to know so they can learn it for the next test.

I explain that my telling them what I want them to know doesn't give any long-term understanding. It might not even provide adequate under-standing to give explanations for the questions I ask on a test. Telling the

Teacher Research

students concepts does not ensure that they will make logical connections and develop understanding. They will memorize facts. It would be easy to give a brief lecture connecting the idea of the net force and inertia to teach about why all objects fall at the same rate in a vacuum. It seems more effective for long-term understanding to experiment with inertia in a horizontal situation with carts and develop some understanding about the relationship between the net force on an object, its mass, and its acceleration. When we then think of the carts falling in a vertical situation, the students can make a logical jump to what is happening here. I frequently have related an anecdote about my fear of flying. When I had done some experiments showing the effect of the force of air upward on an object and had discussions about it, it seemed reasonable to accept that the airplane could, in fact, be supported by the air and thus stay up there. I consider this understanding of the physics concepts to be empowerment relative to the world around me.

Another aspect of teaching through inquiry is its effectiveness in reaching students with very different learning styles and very different abilities. High achievers can hone their skills in critical thinking and asking questions. They can work with others and practice the questioning process to assist others to follow the logic of an argument. They can take the concept to the next step of application and find out more about an aspect of physics. The academically less-able student can also be successful in an inquiry classroom. Because everyone's opinion is valued, there is a safe situation for putting forth arguments, which may or may not be valid. It doesn't matter, because preinstruction activities are voicing what people think about a situation. Observations are valid, and students can observe at many different levels. Understanding the big idea of the unit can happen at different levels as indicated with Dr. Minstrell's rubrics for physics concepts (Minstrell 1989). Some of my students who had not been successful in science classes thrived in the atmosphere provided by inquiry teaching. Academically gifted students with curiosity can also thrive in the inquiry classroom. As our class sizes increase, knowing we have a method of teaching that can reach all students is encouraging.

The Importance of Asking Questions

A goal for all teachers is helping students become lifelong learners. What isn't clear is exactly what that means. What is required of a person to be labeled a *lifelong learner*? Certainly curiosity would be a requirement. If one has no curiosity about the world around him or her, there is no impetus for learning. If there is curiosity, there are questions. How do we encourage students to ask questions? Does the process of teaching with inquiry encourage questioning by the students? Do they refine their questions until they have a question that is doable? Are they asking the question they need to achieve the learning they are seeking? Is the question broad enough to encompass what they have a curiosity for, yet narrow enough to achieve? Formulating a good question is the hard part. A journal enables the students to reflect on their understanding and encourages the formulation of more questions and better questions. Encouraging student questions seems to foster more curiosity and more questions. They become more reflective about the world around them.

How do we foster curiosity with our students? Many come to our classrooms with unbounded curiosity, while many don't appear to care. What happens to the curiosity of students as they move from kindergarten to 12th grade? Have we encouraged their questioning? Have we fostered that desire to explore their world that all children are born with? If, somewhere in the years of school, the questioning and curiosity have disappeared, what can we do to help them regain it? I would suggest we start with teachers who have a passion for what they are teaching. A teacher with a passion for physics increases the chances that students will build upon what curiosity they have about physics and move forward with it. And a teacher with a passion for mathematics or literature or art will impart that passion to students.

Teachers as Reflective Inquirers

When we consider the structure of an inquiry unit, we find many situations for teacher reflection. Assuming we start with a preinstruction activity, what are the initial ideas the students have about this topic? Teachers need to consider what question will start students delving into what they believe about the topic. Once the question is asked, the teacher needs to analyze what the students are thinking and develop activities that address preconceptions and provide observation of results that direct students to the scientifically correct big ideas. What activities would best lead the students to the big ideas of this unit? What data could the students gather to help them see relationships? What activities could provide application and pulling together of the big ideas of this unit?

When discussing the observations, the teacher needs to consider the best questions to ask, the ones that lead the logical thinking of students. How do we best get from observations to conclusions? What questions logically follow the comments each student offers? Has each student followed the logical sequence of ideas to reach the desired conclusion? Has the class come to consensus on the big idea of this unit? Each of these steps requires intense reflection by the teacher.

When the conclusion is reached, the teacher uses reflection to find the questions that best assess the understanding of the students. What are the rubrics that need to be considered when reviewing the student responses? Are there questions on the assessment tool that assess basic understanding, as well as questions to assess understanding for greater application?

Teacher Research

Does the assessment tool require students to stretch their thinking and explain their evidence for an answer? Good questions require the students to reflect on their understanding, and they help students pull their ideas together. Could the reflection on the question create an "aha" response as it helps the student make connections in their understanding?

The Student as Reflective Inquirer

Reflection for students starts with the preinstruction activity. "What do I know or think about this situation?" Here the student needs to consider thoughtfully what he or she believes about the situation. During the activities for development of ideas, students need much reflection to make good observations and then try to make logical connections or meaning. Here again, reflection by the student should consider the big idea that connects the observations or data. During the classroom discussion to reach consensus about the big idea, the student needs to be reflective about the comments of other students and consider if those arguments are valid and support the evidence.

Reflecting Throughout the Process

It is clear that the processes of teaching and learning for understanding require reflection from start to finish. Teaching for student understanding requires the teacher to provide situations and strategies from which students can develop ideas and make sense of the evidence provided. Developing those situations and strategies requires intentional reflection by the teacher on where the students are in their understanding and on how to move their thinking to the next level. Students must take responsibility for their learning. They must remain focused and critically think about their observations and evidence for their conclusions to develop scientifically correct understanding. The effort required from the teacher and the students to intentionally reflect is rewarded by the satisfaction of student understanding and can put students on the path to being lifelong learners.

Reflections

In Chapter 3, Trisha Kagey Boswell described her experiences as a first-year teacher conducting an inquiry into her practice as her students conduct an inquiry on electricity. Here, Dorothy describes her experiences as a veteran teacher conducting an inquiry into her practice as her students learn physics through inquiry. Dorothy writes, "It is very difficult, if not impossible, for K–12 classroom teachers to do the kind of research university people do" (p. 94). She cites the constraints of lack of time, lack of resources, and lack of help. As a teacher with years of classroom experience, and with the "privilege and luxury of having two mentor teachers encouraging my intentional reflections about my teaching" (p. 95), she proposes a way in which a classroom teacher can take the elements of research and make use of them in a sustainable, teacher-friendly way.

Dorothy describes a practice she calls intentional reflection in which a teacher sets aside time, right after teaching, to write in a journal, simultaneously collecting evidence from teaching, making sense of that evidence, and developing questions to guide improvements in teaching. Dorothy is a teacher speaking to other teachers about the value of using the elements of research. These elements can improve the quality of instruction and help us sustain ourselves as professionals, with the satisfaction of knowing we are growing in our ability to teach well.

References

McDermott, L. C. 1984. Research on conceptual understanding in mechanics. *Physics Today* 37: 24–32.

Minstrell, J. 1989. Teaching science for understanding. In *Toward the thinking curriculum: Current cognitive research, 1989 Yearbook*, eds. L. B. Resnick and L. E. Klopfer, 131–149. Alexandria, VA: Association for Supervision and Curriculum Development.

Minstrell, J. 2001. Facets of students' thinking: Designing to cross the gap from research to standards-based practice. In *Designing for science: Implications for everyday, classroom and professional settings*. eds. K. Crowley, C. D. Schunn, T. Okada, 415–444. Mahwah, NJ: Lawrence Erlbaum.

National Research Council (NRC). 1996. *National Science Education Standards*. Washington, DC: National Academy Press.

Simpson, D. 1992, August. Encouraging girls in physics. Presented at the American Association of Physics Teachers summer meeting, Vancouver, B.C.

Simpson, D. 1997. Collaborative conversations: Strategies for engaging students in productive dialogues. *The Science Teacher* 64(8): 40–43.

van Zee, E. H., and J. Minstrell. 1997. Reflective discourse: Developing shared understandings in a physics classroom. *International Journal of Science Education* 19: 209–228.

Chapter 10

Becoming a Teacher Researcher: Giving Space, Finding Space

Christopher Horne

Christopher Horne is a teacher specialist for elementary science for Frederick County, Maryland, public schools and an adjunct professor in the education department at Mount Saint Mary's University in Emmitsburg, Maryland. He is pursuing a doctoral degree in elementary science education at the University of Maryland, College Park. As a science specialist, Chris frequently demonstrates inquiry-based instruction in elementary classrooms. Chris describes a process in which he uses students' written responses during one session as the "text" for reading and discussion during subsequent sessions while he engages fourth-grade students in learning about space science. Then he steps back and reflects upon his experiences in learning to document student thinking.

This chapter has three parts: The first part is about a study, "Giving Children Space," that I have been conducting in fourth-grade classrooms for several years; the second part, "Finding Space," is about doing that study, about becoming a teacher researcher; the third part, "Giving Space, Finding Space," reflects upon these teaching and researching experiences.

Giving Children Space

What is inquiry-based science? What are some effective examples of inquiry-based science? What is the best format for utilizing inquiry-based science? These are just some of the questions my elementary-science-methods students wrote in response to an article in *Science and Children* entitled, "Me, Teach Science?" (Jesky-Smith 2002). Their questions are well worth considering. In survey responses conducted by Jesky-Smith, "When asked to define inquiry-based science, 46% of the students simply stated that they did not know or left the item blank" (p. 29).

The National Science Education Standards (NRC 1996) clearly advocate an emphasis on inquiry-based science:

- Inquiry into authentic questions generated from student experiences is the central strategy for teaching science (p. 31).

- Science as inquiry is basic to science education and a controlling principle in the ultimate organization and selection of students' activities (p. 105).
- Inquiry is a critical component of a science program at all grade levels and in every domain of science ... (p. 214).

Words such as *central, basic,* and *critical* suggest that inquiry is undeniably at the heart of good science teaching and learning. But the essential question still remains unanswered: What is inquiry-based science? According to the Standards: Inquiry is a set of interrelated processes by which scientists and students pose questions about the natural world and investigate phenomena; in doing so, students acquire knowledge and develop rich understanding of concepts, principles, models, and theories (p. 214).

So, inquiry begins when we pose questions. We pose questions because we wonder. Our wonder sometimes prompts us to respond through investigation. Our investigation allows us to acquire knowledge. This knowledge leads us to pose more questions. As we inquire, as we wonder, as we investigate, we develop a richer understanding.

During one school year, I adopted several practices with a group of fourth-grade students in our study of space science that have engaged us in a practice of wondering, questioning, and investigating—the process of inquiry.

Begin With "I Wonder"

I have had a lifelong love of science and continue to wonder and question as I ponder the complexities of the universe. But, when I meet a group of students for the first time, I am quite certain they have little desire to listen at length to my interests and questions. Students are, however, excited to share their own interests and ponder their own questions, if given the opportunity. I start each science unit with the question, "What do you wonder?" and allow the children time to discuss in small groups, before each writes an individual response. Students posed these and other questions as we began our unit on space:
- How does a meteor shower happen?
- Can we inhabit Mars?
- How do the stars transform into things like the Big Dipper and the Little Dipper?
- How come planets with rings have them?
- Why don't the planets just fall out of space?
- Why isn't there any oxygen in space?

Respecting student questions and listening to their wonderings encourages them to take my questions more seriously. I have adopted the practice of maintaining a list of student questions and answers throughout the unit with a stated goal of posing more questions than we answer.

Teacher Research

Moving Toward Inquiry

At the start of a unit or lesson I often ask my fourth-grade students to give a written response to a content-related question. For example, in September I posed the question, "Why does it get dark at night?" Responses to the question helped me to understand the students' level of understanding so I could effectively address their specific needs.

It occurred to me that, rather than simply using the information from their responses to drive *my* instruction, I could reproduce the students' responses and distribute them during a subsequent lesson so that *their* ideas would be the central driving force of the unit.

During my next meeting with the class I distributed all 28 responses to the question in typewritten form and allowed time for the students to read and consider their classmates' ideas. I asked them to pick at least one idea with which they agreed or disagreed and to be ready to discuss their reasons for supporting or rejecting the statement. Each of the responses was numbered for easy identification, and no names were used. In this way we could talk freely about ideas rather than considering personalities. The results were extremely encouraging. The students were engaged in animated dialogue—evidence they enjoy talking about their ideas. They were quickly willing to make statements and support them with explanations. They also had no trouble respectfully disagreeing with one another and stating reasons for their beliefs.

After distributing the students' responses, our conversation got underway:

Sarah: I disagree with number 19 [*19:* When the Sun goes down then the Moon comes up. Then it gets dark.] because when we're having—when it's night the Moon is blocking the Sun—when it's daytime the Sun is blocking the Moon.
Mr. Horne: So, at nighttime, the Moon is blocking the Sun?
Sarah: [Nods head, indicating "yes."]
Shaan: I disagree with Sarah because if the Moon blocks the Sun, that's a solar eclipse, and we don't have eclipses every month.
Mr. Horne: What do you mean, *solar eclipse?*
Shaan: That's when the Moon comes in front of the Sun ...
Natasha: I agree with Shaan because if the Moon was blocking the Sun, where would the Sun be the other half of the day?

The conversation continued in this manner for some time. Initially, it was somewhat surprising to me that fourth-grade students would engage in such a lively discussion. In retrospect, it makes sense. Too often, as teachers, we tell things to students without allowing time for them to share their ideas. When given the time and opportunity, students will openly and eagerly share their thinking. Initially, the most difficult aspect of this process was to step back from the conversation and allow the students to communicate their ideas to one another without interfering (see Gallas 1995; van Zee et al. 2001). The teacher's role during the discussion should be to clarify statements made by students and to facilitate the discussion. In this way, the students remain at the center of the conversation.

It was exciting to me to realize that, through this process, students were engaged in scientific inquiry in a number of ways. Through this simple activity, they were posing questions to one another, they were analyzing alternative explanations for scientific phenomena, and they were communicating scientific arguments—all based on an analysis of their own ideas.

Continuing the Process

Throughout the remainder of the school year, I used this strategy with the students with some variations. When I asked the students to respond to the question, "Why does the Moon change the way it looks?" I studied their responses and decided to produce a much shorter list of four representative statements:

1 I think the Moon changes because the clouds cover it up. That is why I think the Moon changes the way it looks.
2 The Moon changes the way it looks because the Sun shines on it, and the Moon is revolving around the Earth so the Sun shines on different parts of the Moon.
3 The Moon changes because the Earth blocks the light from the Sun and doesn't put as much sunlight on to the Moon, so it makes a pattern.
4 The Moon changes the way it looks because, when the Sun goes down, then the Moon changes shapes. It matters how hot the Sun was that day.

During our next class meeting, I distributed the list to each student, gave them several minutes to read the statements, then allowed them time to support or refute the ideas in small groups. This was an important variation in a number of ways. The shorter list gave them less data to analyze and the small-cooperative-group setting provided more opportunities for students to talk and express their thinking in a setting less intimidating than that of the whole class. Following the small-group discussion, a representative from each group shared an important aspect of their conversation with the class.

In subsequent meetings, I provided opportunities for the students to (1) work with physical models, (2) make repeated observations of the Moon in the sky and on the internet, and (3) watch the Moon change position in the sky throughout the afternoon during the school day.

After giving my students several weeks of hands-on experiences with physical models and opportunities to analyze data and make observations over time, I felt it would again be useful to ask them to write their responses to the original question, "Why does the Moon change the way it looks?" This feedback would help me to see how their thinking had changed and also serve as a means of giving them access to each other's ideas (see Horne 1999).

This time I tried another variation to promote inquiry. Based on the students' written responses, I compiled a representative list of five varying ideas and distributed them during our next lesson. I asked my students to read the list, select one idea, and describe, in writing, evidence to support their choice. I also gave them the option of including a picture. After about 10 minutes, I invited them to share their responses with one another in a whole-group format.

The conversation that followed was a dynamic interaction of students sharing ideas and points of view. Controversy arose over the specific meaning of the wording of the question, "Why does the Moon change the way it looks?" The argument stemmed from a discussion they had concerning Statement 4, which said, "The Moon changes the way it looks because of the time of day it is." This statement was probably based upon observations we made in class one afternoon while noting the change in orientation the waxing crescent Moon was making in the sky. One student argued that the intent of the question was to address the changing phase of the Moon, not its orientation. More than four minutes of discussion that I did not interrupt ensued. A small portion of the conversation is transcribed here:

Sean: Say the Moon was a person, if it did a cartwheel, would it be changing the way it looks?

Several voices: Yes.

Obella: Okay, let's say I was the Moon and I standed on my head. You are saying that I would look the same to you?

Sean: I'm saying you wouldn't look the same to me.

Obella: That's exactly what you're saying.

Alyssa: He would be the same person as stood up, except to other people looking at him he would look different.

Sean: He just changed position; he didn't change the way he looks.

This conversation was exciting for a number of reasons. I was pleased that I had been able to step aside and let the students engage in an extended dialogue without feeling it necessary to include me—a practice van Zee and colleagues (2001) call "spontaneous student-generated inquiry discussion." The students were engaged in the process of thinking about a question critically and logically. They were spontaneously posing questions to one another. They were formulating explanations for their ideas. They were doing inquiry!

How Do You Begin?

For a recent assignment, a preservice teacher wrote

> If a science class is to be driven by the inquiring of the students, how do you begin? As a teacher, show me how to do this. Preservice teachers are more than eager and willing to learn. Give us the tools to do it.

Student involvement is at the heart of inquiry-based science. The most important thing you can bring to the classroom is a commitment to allowing students time to wonder, time to consider their own questions, and time to verbally interact with one another. Time to wonder followed by a cycle of writing, reading, and responding can be a great way to promote inquiry in your classroom. And, while the students are actively engaged in dialogue, you can be actively engaged in thinking about their thinking. Try it—inquiry will happen!

Finding Space

- New Orleans
- Philadelphia
- Atlanta
- Saint Louis
- Dallas
- The National Association of Research in Science Teaching Conference
- The National Science Teachers Association Conference
- The Maryland Association of Science Teachers Conference
- The Ethnography in Education Research Forum
- Examining Teacher's Inquiry Into Student Inquiry in Elementary Science
- Giving Children Space: An Inquiry Into the Minds and Hearts of Fourth Graders in the Space Science Classroom
- BYOD (Bring Your Own Data): A Look at Video, Audio, Transcripts, and Student Work as a Starting Point for Teacher Research into Student Thinking
- Thinking About Student Thinking: A Plan for Developing a Student-Centered, Inquiry-Based Classroom
- Case Studies of Student Inquiry in Physical Science
- Analyzing Student Thinking: A Look at Video, Audio, Transcripts, and Student
- Work as a Starting Point for Teacher Research

What is it like to travel to so many locations? To attend so many conferences? To present in so many forums? What is it like to have such a rich array of experiences?

To meet so many people who are so committed to excellence in education? To learn from professionals and experts in teaching, learning, and research?

The experience of attending and presenting at so many conferences has been life changing. I am humbled. I recognize that all my efforts, all my insights, all my research is but one small part of a great picture. But I do not feel insignificant. As I grow, my understanding deepens, my teaching is enriched, my students are blessed. And perhaps others grow as a result of my sharing.

I continue to question. I continue to wonder, I continue to ask. Sometimes the answers come. Sometimes confusion reigns. Still, I press forward, with hope, enthusiastically searching and re-searching. Here is a statement that captures well what I have experienced:

> There is no such thing as teaching without research and research without teaching. One inhabits the body of the other. As I teach, I continue to search and re-search. I teach because I search, because I question, and because I submit myself to questioning. I research because I notice things, take cognizance of them. And in so doing, I intervene. And intervening, I educate and educate myself. I do research so as to know what I do not yet know and to communicate and proclaim what I discover (Freire 1998, p. 35).

NSTA Teacher Researcher Day

The National Science Teachers Association (NSTA) has sponsored Teacher Researcher Day for the past several years during their annual conference. It has been my pleasure to participate in each of these events. During the 2004 NSTA conference in Atlanta, Georgia, I was asked to speak on a panel of teacher researchers during the second annual Teacher Researcher Day. The description of the session stated that, "A panel of researchers will share their insights and experiences in inquiring about their students' science learning."

The invitation to speak provided an opportunity to reflect on the impact of my experiences as a teacher researcher, especially since my admission to the University of Maryland in the fall of 1999. I was given five minutes to "tell my story." Where should I begin? What important points I should share? Who is the audience? Why will they want to hear from me? My mind raced. My experience has been so rich—there is so much to tell. But, what is relevant to an audience of teacher researchers? My questions remained, but the time to speak arrived. So I began:

> When I started this work, I had an idea about being a teacher researcher and the notion of reflective teaching and I was really looking at things from the perspective of, "What kind of innovations could really make a

difference for students?" And so the work, that I have titled now, "Giving Children Space," is a bit of a play on words and what I really initially wanted to do was give children space in the sense of content knowledge. And I believed that if I did the right things and knew the right methods and techniques, that I could really transfer a lot of great knowledge that I had over to these students.

I wanted the audience to recognize that my earlier views of research consisted of developing an innovation, implementing the innovation, and then measuring the impact of the innovation. This was to change.

Five years has taught me a lot. I have learned and grown over the years and paid attention to what I've been noticing. I actually had a plan to look "for" certain things when I started my work. And now, year after year going back into fourth-grade classrooms and working with these fourth graders, instead of looking "for," I am more looking "at" what the students are presenting. I'm seeing a huge shift in the way I've been thinking.

In my work with hundreds of elementary classroom teachers and preservice teachers over the past decade, I have noted a commonly held paradigm for the concept of research—one quite similar to the views I held before beginning my doctoral studies. It has been my hope and goal to broaden that view by sharing openly the exciting work I have taken part in as a teacher specialist and teacher researcher in the elementary school. Perhaps my short talk could open the minds and hearts of teachers to think more openly about their role as a teacher researcher in their classrooms. By suggesting varied means of data collection and analysis, and an emphasis on reflection, I hope to inspire and encourage teachers to consider themselves teacher researchers and begin the hard and exciting work of examining one's own teaching.

The means by which I've been collecting data is doing videotape, audiotape, and taking these tapes and transcribing them, analyzing what the students are saying, thinking about what they are saying, interviewing students, collecting student work, reading over what they are saying, and on top of that just keeping a journal and watching and noticing how I'm changing, how my thinking is changing. There have been a lot of, I think, notable changes in my own understandings over time and it's been through just really paying attention to students. I used to be much more teacher centered. I'm seeing a shift to be more student centered. I used to be more, the sage on the stage, now I'm more the guide on the side. Rather than saying a lot and having a lot to say, I'm learning to stop talking so much and listen to what the students have to say. Pay close attention to what to they have to say. Then, use that kind of understanding to change my instruction.

Teacher Research

My shift from a more teacher-centered approach to a more student-centered approach would not have happened, could not have happened, without a commitment to listening closely to children and looking carefully at the classroom from the students' point of view. As a teacher researcher, I cannot simply look at the practice and consider how the students need to change, but rather, I must look deeply at my own practice through the lens of the student and consider how I need to change. This, it seems to me, is the starting point of teacher research. But reflection is only one piece. Teacher researchers must also be committed to "doing something" in response to their discoveries and be willing to share their insights with others. In a small way, I have been able to share my discoveries and insights through events such as the NSTA Teacher Researcher Day.

To conclude my comments at the Teacher Researcher Day in Atlanta, I shared these insights:

> So, what I have come to find out is that now I have a title for my work, that I call "Giving Children Space," but rather than giving them space in the sense of content knowledge, I am giving them space, the mental space, the emotional space to ask questions, to talk to one another, to actually do inquiry. And I pay attention and listen. And then, miraculously, as I give children space, they, in turn, come to have, bring an understanding of content knowledge, which has been an exciting thing to see.

Giving Space, Finding Space

Giving children space requires a commitment to surrendering some control in the classroom. Giving space means giving up something. Perhaps something held very dear, like a need for control, or simply an old habit or old belief that has become automatic. A good friend once asked me to design a button for a kindergarten curriculum workshop. The phrase to be incorporated onto the button was: "Let Go … the Children Will Catch You!" I found a picture of a bewildered-looking person hanging from a rope. Underneath I placed a picture of happy children with their hands in the air, seemingly ready to offer their support when needed. The phrase and design had quite an impact on me. It is so easy to hold on to old ways, to clutch tightly to control, and to insist upon being the dominant voice of the classroom. Creating the button allowed me to see myself.

Through the practice of looking closely at my own teaching, I have learned to start to let go and give children space. In so doing, I have seen the power of conducting my own classroom research. As I let go of my firm grip on old practices and accept the possibility of new paradigms, a large new world of teaching, learning, and researching has opened for me. Through careful and thoughtful research I am not only giving space, I am finding it.

Reflections

Like Trisha Kagey Boswell (Chapter 3) and Dorothy Simpson (Chapter 9), Chris was a teacher doing an inquiry into his students' inquiry. First he shows us what happened in his classroom as he listened to his students talk to one another about the Moon. He describes how he tried to stay out of their way so that they could have a conversation and learn from one another. Then he tells us how he, as a teacher, gradually came to teach in this way. He writes, "When I started the work, I had an idea about being a teacher researcher and the notion of reflective teaching and I was really looking at things from the perspective of 'What kind of innovations could really make a difference for students?'" (p. 106). But over years of doing teacher research, his view has changed. "I actually had a plan to look 'for' certain things when I started my work. And now … I am looking 'at' what the students are presenting" (p. 107).

Collecting evidence, making sense of the evidence, and taking seriously what he learned from that evidence to inform his teaching, Chris tells us he has learned "… to stop talking so much and listen to what the students have to say. Pay close attention to what they have to say. Then use that kind of understanding to change my instruction" (p. 107). Teacher research has transformed his view of teaching and learning. Doing teacher research has also transformed his view of the nature of teacher research itself.

References

Freire, P. 1998. *Pedagogy of freedom: Ethics, democracy, and civic courage.* Lanham, MD: Rowman and Littlefield.

Gallas, K. 1995. *Talking their way into science.* New York: Teachers College Press.

Horne, C. 1999. Using Moon models: Is "hands-on" really enough? Maryland Association of Science *Teachers Rapper* 24 (4): 17–20.

Jesky-Smith, R. 2002. Me, teach science? *Science and Children* 39 (6): 26–31.

National Research Council (NRC). 1996. *National Science Education Standards.* Washington, DC: National Academy Press.

van Zee, E. H., M. Iwasyk, A. Kurose, D. Simpson, and J. Wild. 2001. Student and teacher questioning during conversations about science. *Journal of Research in Science Teaching* 38 (2): 159–190.

Teachers Supporting Teachers in Learning

Diantha Lay

Diantha Lay is principal of an elementary school in Montgomery County, Maryland. When she wrote this chapter, she was just start- ing a new position for the county as a staff development teacher. Earlier she had been a second- and a fourth-grade teacher with a passion for science. When her county decided to establish the new position of staff development teacher in every school, Diantha em- barked on a new adventure. In this chapter, she describes the for- mation of teacher study groups as she began to engage colleagues in developing a professional learning community in their school.

Change is everywhere. It is all around us. It is ever present in our lives. In no other profession is change more apparent than in the field of edu- cation. We are standing on the threshold of many important changes in our educational system. I happen to be planted on the precipice of that change. There is not a road map, there is not a precedent, and there is not a book to follow. There is a vision. There is research. There is funding. My school district believes that professional learning should take place within the school site and with colleagues. Professional learning should occur frequently throughout the school day. Research shows that learning that takes place at workshops or conferences, while interesting and motivating, rarely transfers into the classroom to affect the daily work of teachers and students (McLaughlin and Talbert 1993, p. 84). Although this study was confined to secondary schools, it makes sense that the findings would apply to elementary schools as well.

In schools with collaborative professional learning communities, teach- ers receive the support needed to learn new practices. This learning en- ables students to meet higher standards of achievement. Teachers sup- porting teachers in learning new strategies, joint planning, and solving common instructional problems should lead to increased student learning in virtually any setting (McLaughlin and Talbert 1993, p. 89). So what does this mean for my school district, my school, and me?

County Establishes New Position of Staff Development Teacher

Enter the staff development teacher—me. I am a conduit of change within my school system. My district has put big bucks on the line in the form of the staff development teacher. The new position of staff development teacher has been allocated to every school in my county, a total of 179 schools. The role of the staff development teacher is to facilitate building professional learning communities within the school setting. Job-embedded learning is learning by doing, reflecting on the experience, and then generating and sharing new insights and learning with others.

It is my role to develop, establish, and support these professional learning communities. As a part of our new county initiatives, teachers are required to develop a professional development plan. Many options are available for professional development, and these options were presented to the staff during an inservice training. One option was a study group. Teachers were interested in developing various study groups within the school. A study group is probably the most frequently discussed option for job-embedded learning. Groups of teachers come together to learn more about a particular topic. The group reviews and discusses literature, visits model programs, and meets to discuss the potential of the practices or program for the school (Wood and McQuarrie 1999, p. 10). Dennis Sparks, executive director of the National Staff Development Council, remarked that collaboration is perhaps the most effective form of staff development. According to his organization, "one of the most obvious and direct ways to improve teaching is to have teachers continuously work with others to improve the quality of their lessons and to examine student work to determine whether those lessons are assisting all students to achieve at all levels." Teachers collaborating, sharing, and observing is exactly what is taking place in my building. The idea is to build a community and culture that helps educators gain new knowledge that can make a difference in their work.

Formation of a Study Group

The first study group to form was a group of reading initiative (RI) teachers who provided special reading instruction and support to small groups of primary students. These teachers are highly respected by staff members, and they generated excitement about forming this group and having a study group as a part of their professional development plan. It just took spreading the word before other groups of teachers were exploring the idea of a study group as well. The RI teachers decided to meet weekly during lunch to discuss what they were doing with their classes and to exchange ideas. They also wanted to visit each others' classrooms during instructional time to gain insight on teaching strategies. After an observation, a veteran teacher remarked, "I can't believe how much I learned in a 30-minute time block. She is a phenomenal teacher and has so much to share. I can't believe that I've been teaching down the hall from her for three years, and I've never watched her teach. What a great experience. Thank you."

The RI Study Group then selected *Strategies That Work* (Harvey and Goudvis 2000) as a book club book. They read the book and selected a strategy a month. They took the strategy into their classroom and tried it out. After experimenting with the strategy, they came together and discussed what they did, what they would do differently, and improvements they would make. This learning experience was an invaluable part of their instruction. But the proof of their efforts was in the results from the students. Quarterly assessments had just been completed for the second marking period. Students in the reading initiative classes improved in their reading skills an average of 18%, almost double what the RI classes had attained in the past. The only variable in the instruction was that the RI teachers were talking, sharing, and observing instructional practices. They felt that the study group was a vital and important part of student achievement.

A Study Group With a Focus on Questioning

The second study group that formed was the Governor's Academy (GA) Group. This group of teachers had attended the Governor's Academy for Math and Science for a six-week period during the summer and wanted to continue to work on a project they had developed then. These teachers came from different grade levels and did not have a common lunch or planning time, so they decided to meet after school each week to work on their project and to share practices across grade levels. Their mission was to look at their own practice as it related to math and science.

The group decided that they wanted to focus on the kinds of questions that they asked. They observed each other and kept a tally of the kinds of questions. The results were a surprise. They adapted a grid from *Teaching from a Research Knowledge Base* (Bellon et al. 1996), which looks at the purposes of questions. Questions fell into four categories: instructing, assessing, managing, and promoting cognitive engagement. The study group found that 75% of the questions teachers asked were managing the environment (maintaining attention and controlling behavior) and promoting engagement (encouraging involvement). Teachers were not assessing nor were they questioning as a part of instruction. They developed strategies to modify types of questions that they asked their students and tracked changes in their questioning practices. One teacher said, "I had no idea that I asked so many meaningless questions and that my instruction was weak in the area of questioning. I couldn't believe that so few higher-order questions were asked."

One teacher asked for further assistance from a peer. Ms. K agreed to come in and lead a discussion with a science class on the subject of structures. The observing teacher made a note of every question that Ms. K asked. The following are some questions asked during a class discussion:

- Why do you think that?
- How do you know it will work that way?
- What do you think would happen if the base changed?
- Does anyone have any other ideas as to how it would work?
- Can you explain that again?

After the class, the observing teacher noted, "I was surprised at the level of questions that were generated in the class. The teacher only acted as a facilitator to generate more discussion within the class. I come from the 'direct instruction' model, and all of this is foreign to me. I had no idea that a science class could run that way." The two teachers continued their dialogue, and co-teaching of science resulted in more collaborative teaching.

Reflecting on the Study-Group Process

Teachers are assessing what students are learning and are basing instruction on data that they have collected. They are learning that some of the most important resources are right at their fingertips, next door, or across the hall. There is excitement in the new wave of instruction and teaching. Teachers are talking about student work and sharing ideas. They are meeting regularly to discuss instructional practices and strategies.

Study groups are in their infancy in our school. We have just begun a process that is an important part of our professional development. Teachers' attitudes toward change and commitment to student learning are key ingredients in achieving a new way of looking at professional development. Important learning communities are formed, and important changes result. The support given in study groups is ongoing and focused on improving student achievement.

According to Roland Barth (2000), a school that has a strong context for change resembles a *community of learners*. He describes a learning community as "a place where all participants—teachers, principals, parents, and students—engage in learning and teaching." We are teaching ourselves. We are discovering best practices from experts in our field and in our building. As we move forward in a new kind of learning community, we are discovering that professional development is about change. We are experiencing change in what we know and believe about teaching and learning and what we can do in the classroom, which will result in increasing student achievement.

Chapter 11

Reflections

In previous chapters, many teachers have written about their individual inquiries. Teacher research groups are powerful places for sharing and collaborating when individual teachers seek support as they pursue this challenging work. But, by its nature, teacher research is the kind of work chosen by an individual for his or her own reasons. A principal or staff development teacher who decided to implement a teacher-research group as a professional development program would probably encounter resistance. In this chapter, Diantha has invited the teachers at her school, as one option for professional development, to form a study group of their own choosing. The teachers who formed the Governor's Academy Group decided they wanted "to look at their own practice as it related to math and science."

The activities chosen by this group correspond to the elements of teacher research. They engaged in questioning: They wanted to know more about the kinds of questions they were asking in class. They collected evidence, by observing each other and tallying the kinds of questions asked. That they chose to do this shows a high level of trust and sharing among the group members. They made sense of the evidence and chose to ask one another to come in and model questioning for them. Throughout the process, sharing is apparent. Diantha's inclusive view of teacher research made it possible for the teachers at her school to use these elements for their own purposes. The result is increased collaboration and learning for these teachers.

References

Barth, R. 2000. Building a community of learners. *Principal* 79(4): 68–69.

Bellon, J., E. C. Bellon, and M. A. Blank. 1996. *Teaching from a research knowledge base: A development and renewal process.* Upper Saddle River, NJ: Prentice-Hall.

Harvey, S., and A. Goudvis. 2000. *Strategies that work: Teaching comprehension to enhance understanding.* Portland, ME: Stenhouse.

McLaughlin, M., and J. Talbert. 1993. *Contexts that matter for teaching and learning.* Palo Alto, CA: Stanford University Center for Research on the Context of Secondary School Teaching. (ERIC Document Reproduction Service ED357023)

Sparks, D. 2002. *Designing powerful professional development for teachers and principals.* Oxford, OH: National Staff Development Council (ED 470239).

Wood, F. H., and F. McQuarrie Jr. 1999. On-the-job learning. *Journal of Staff Development* (Summer) 20 (3): 10–13.

Chapter 12

TEAM Connections:
Four Teachers' Journeys Into Action Research

Judy Fix, Norma Fletcher, Dianne Johnson, and Janet Siulc

Judy Fix is principal of Bennett Park Montessori Center #32, a public preK-to-eighth-grade school in Buffalo, New York. At the time this research occurred, she was a multiage (PreK/K) Montessori Teacher at Bennett Park. She continues to be a strong proponent of action research, now as an administrator, and encourages new Montessori teachers to explore the benefits of action research.

Norma Fletcher has retired from the Buffalo public schools but continues to work as a mathematics coach for Buffalo teachers, as a supervisor and instructor for prospective elementary school teachers at Buffalo State College, and as manager of a comprehensive school reform grant. When this report was written, she was program coordinator for the Stanley M. Makowski Early Childhood Center.

Dianne Johnson is a multiage teacher for grades 5 and 6 at an arts magnet school, Waterfront Elementary School, in Buffalo. She first collaborated with Judy Fix in finding out about action research and eventually with their colleagues, Janet and Norma, in the Teacher Education at the Museum (TEAM) project.

Janet Siulc is the special education coordinator at Enterprise Charter School in Buffalo. When this paper was written, she was a special education resource room teacher in the Buffalo public schools, from which she retired in 2004.

This group of teachers in the Buffalo Public School District wondered what they could do that would go beyond talk and speculation about their teaching practices. They wanted to take action in their classrooms. This chapter is about the journey upon which the four teachers embarked as they hoped to find out if what they thought they were doing was really making a difference in their students' learning.

We have all heard the rumors about teachers who, at the beginning of each school year, merely change the dates in their old plan books and teach the same lessons they have always taught in their classrooms. Our experience has been that these teachers are not the norm. The teachers we know are constantly reflecting on and evaluating their own teaching practice. These teachers routinely talk about classroom methods that work or don't work, always with the hope of improving student learning and achievement. It's important to talk about practice, but a group of teachers in the Buffalo, New York, Public School District wondered what we could do that would go beyond talk and speculation. We wanted to take action in our classrooms. This article is about the journey that four of us embarked upon as we hoped to find out if what we thought we were doing was really making a difference.

How We Met

Our journey has its roots in the early 1990s at TEAM (Teacher Education at the Museum), a local systemic change project funded by the National Science Foundation (Dow 1991, 1993). The goal of TEAM is to educate teachers in inquiry-based methods of science education through hands-on kit activities and other advanced professional development opportunities. The four of us are part of a group of teacher leaders for TEAM, where we help to plan and teach the professional development courses for preK-through-eighth-grade teachers in the Buffalo Public School District.

We are also full-time classroom teachers, and, as we worked together on TEAM projects, we learned quite a lot about one another. We are all teachers in the same urban school district, but our individual teaching situations are unique. Our group includes Norma, a program coordinator for an early childhood center; Jan, a special education resource teacher at a neighborhood school; Dianne, a fifth-and-sixth-grade teacher at an arts magnet; and Judy, a preK/K Montessori teacher. Our group may represent four different schools and four different grade levels, but one important and binding commonality holds us together. We are all passionate about teaching and learning through inquiry.

As we met with one another on a regular basis to work on TEAM projects, our relationship evolved. We shared questions and concerns about our own classroom experiences and looked to one another for collegiality and intellectual stimulation. We had quite a few hunches about our classroom practices, but we wanted something more. We wanted to find a vehicle that would help us to examine our hunches.

Teacher
Research

How Action Research Found Us

Our vehicle emerged when Judy was introduced to action research through a project with a student teacher. As part of a university requirement, a student teacher in Judy's school was required to conduct a small action research study. As she worked with this student teacher, Judy discovered that action research could provide her with a means to explore her own classroom hunches. Judy shared her ideas with Dianne, and they both knew that they needed to learn more about action research. With the support of Peter Dow and Cathy Chamberlin, two of the TEAM administrators, Dianne and Judy began reading, looking for models, and trying to educate themselves about the action research process. As they learned more and became excited about the possibilities of action research, other TEAM teacher leaders joined the search, and a study group emerged.

As we studied about action research, we collectively decided upon two guidelines for our own research project. First, we wanted to use authentic objects to stimulate student inquiry. Authentic objects are the items that students find in the real world as opposed to models that only represent these real-world items. The use of authentic objects was a natural extension of our work with TEAM, because we used real objects such as bones, feathers, and pelts in our professional development courses. The bones, pelts, and other objects stimulated many questions for us and the teachers who took the TEAM courses, so we wondered if the objects could inspire our children to ask questions also. We all agreed that inquiry through the use of authentic objects would be the focus for our action research projects.

The second thing we agreed upon was that we wanted to formulate a common question we could each study in our respective classrooms. By this time in our journey, our relationship as a group had evolved into a true collegial learning community. We had already collaborated on many occasions through TEAM, and it seemed natural for us to use our "team connection" for our action research project as well. By studying a common question, we could take advantage of our common interests but still pursue our questions within our own individual classrooms.

We developed several questions and carefully considered each of them, but had some difficulty isolating one specific research question. We realized we needed some expert assistance. We found that expertise in Cathy Battaglia, a principal at a local high school who had completed her doctoral dissertation on the topic of action research. Cathy was willing and eager to work with us, and she helped us to focus our question. After much discussion and deliberation, we decided that our research would consider "In what ways might I promote inquiry using authentic objects as elements of surprise?"

The Action Research Model

The development of a research question is only the first step in an action research project. By definition, research requires a method for systematic data collection and analysis. Kathy showed us a model to use to guide our research project. The Action Research Spiral Model (Kemmis and McTaggert 1988) is an ongoing, reflective action research model. Based upon this model, researchers must first go through a phase called *reconnaissance*. A reconnaissance is a preliminary examination or survey, and, in the case of our action research, the reconnaissance gave us the chance to gather baseline data for future action. Our reconnaissance plan, based upon our research question, was for each of us to place a real mammal skull somewhere in our classrooms and, without any provocation, allow our students to explore the object on their own. What we would learn surprised each of us, and not always in ways that we had hoped.

Like any other research project, our action research required the collection of substantial amounts of data. For this, we relied heavily upon the use of journals. We had been using journals to record our ideas as they related to our work with TEAM. Now, with our action research, our journals took on a new level of importance. Our journals became the place where we reflected and wrote our observations on our action research progress. These data took the form of student responses, our own observations, quotes from others, and reflections and analysis on the research process. In much the same way that other scientific researchers use laboratory journals, our journals would be the cohesive record of evidence for our research journey.

What We Learned

Through our action research, we learned volumes about inquiry and the use of authentic objects. We also learned quite a bit about ourselves in the process. As we reflected upon our journey, three major themes emerged.

It's Okay to Wonder

The first theme to emerge was that the classroom climate influences students' abilities to engage in inquiry. We had hoped that, by placing the skulls in the classroom without any fanfare, the students would show some spontaneous excitement about the object.

But after placing a skull in her classroom during reconnaissance, Jan was surprised when her students completely ignored the skull. She had hoped that her resource room students would find this object fascinating and would be drawn to it immediately. Then she realized that her students had a routine to follow every time they entered the classroom and they needed her permission to deviate from their routine. After she asked the students, "What do you notice? What do you think about it? What do you want to know?" they were full of questions and observations. Jan learned that by asking a few inviting questions, she was able to give her students permission to participate in the inquiry. She had to let them know that it is OK to wonder.

Dianne also had an important realization about how the students can shape the climate of inquiry in the classroom. During reconnaissance, Dianne discovered that her fifth- and sixth-grade students had several questions about the skull, but they were not the kind of questions that she had anticipated. The students' questions centered on deciphering her intention for bringing the skull to their classroom. They were convinced that there were ulterior motives involved. For example, some of the students asked if the skull might have something to do with Groundhog Day because it was February. In this case, Dianne realized that her students' natural curiosity had been tempered by the school culture that seems to require every lesson to have a single, simple answer. She had to teach her savvy students how to re-engage their own curiosity and to explore the object with a fresh and open mind.

Powerful Questions/Powerful Thinking

One of the most important lessons that we learned from our action research journey is that powerful questions are at the heart of inquiry. According to our definition, a powerful question is one that can be investigated and that promotes inquiry. In an inquiry classroom, we learned to recognize when our students asked powerful questions, and, in addition, we learned how to teach our students to ask their own powerful questions. Children typically ask simple questions, such as "Is it real?" or "Is it a dinosaur?" These types of questions are closed-ended, simple requests for information. Powerful questions differ from simple questions because they are based in the child's wonderment about the object. Powerful questions also reveal children's understanding of an object.

As a program coordinator, Norma works with several different preK teachers. She found that the teachers who were using inquiry with authentic objects were excited about their students' growing ability to ask powerful questions—and their own ability to recognize these types of questions. Norma saw her teachers create new learning environments based upon the questions that emerged from the children.

The move from a traditional classroom setting, in which the teacher asks the questions and the students supply the answer, to an inquiry classroom, in which the questions come from student explorations can be quite difficult. To become better inquiry teachers, we had to develop a strategy to elicit powerful questions from our students. We found that by asking open-ended questions, our students supplied rich responses that helped us to understand better what they thought about the object. The questions that we used included:

- What do you see?
- What do you think about these objects? Tell me about them. Draw one.
- Is there one object that you would like to find out more about?

Shedding the Role of "All-Powerful Giver of Information"

When we first began our action research journey, we focused on what we could learn about how our students respond to inquiry. As we learned more about inquiry teaching, we found ourselves also rethinking our own role in the classroom. In traditional, teacher-centered classrooms, the teacher is the authority on knowledge, or, as we describe it, the "All-Powerful Giver of Information." The teacher does most of the talking and the students do the listening. The teacher's role changes when students learn to engage in their own inquiries. In an inquiry classroom, the students ask the questions, and the teacher has to become a better listener and observer.

Judy noticed that, if several of her students asked similar questions, or if the same question seemed to re-emerge, she could structure an investigation to help them to find an answer. In one instance, Judy heard her students asking questions about an object that might be answered with the appropriate tools. As unobtrusively as possible, Judy gathered some magnifying glasses and rulers and placed them in the classroom for student use. By listening, she was able to provide the structure that the students needed without removing the students from the flow of their own exploration.

Jan also had an experience that demonstrated her important new role as classroom observer. While her students were engaged in an exploration of some authentic objects, she noticed that one student was distracted by a piece of bubble wrap that had been used to protect the skull. Jan was able to gently take away the distracting paper, and the student re-engaged with the rest of the group in the inquiry.

As teachers, we had to learn to trust our students to ask powerful questions for themselves at an appropriate time. By listening and observing our students as they engaged in inquiry, we were able to help our students to develop their own understanding of science in a way that fit their specific learning needs. Listening to the conversations among students was as important to the inquiry process as the dialogue between students and teachers.

I Used to Think, and Now I Know

As veteran teachers, we found the process of action research to be both humbling and professionally challenging. We learned a lot about teaching scientific inquiry with authentic objects, our students' responses to inquiry, and the contexts that frame these experiences. We learned as much, if not more, about our own teaching beliefs and philosophies. We have learned that, as a group, we can accomplish great things for our own professional development and for our students' science achievement.

This chapter provides only a brief glimpse into the many places that our action-research journey took us. We hope that other teachers are inspired to begin their own action-research journey that will certainly help to turn their own powerful questions into classroom action.

Reflections

Judy, Norma, Dianne, and Janet began their study with the element of sharing. Their ongoing collaboration and discussion brought them to teacher research. As they studied how to do an action-research project, they were intentional about their process, and used the group as a collective sense-making tool, a way to understand their own thinking. Their collaborative process is a powerful part of their inquiry. They made agreements: "First, we wanted to use authentic objects to stimulate student inquiry" (p. 118). And: "The second thing we agreed upon was that we wanted to formulate a common question that we could each study in our respective classrooms … By studying a common question, we could take advantage of our common interests but still pursue our questions within our own individual classrooms" (p. 118). Built into their process is the idea that they would look at how this inquiry played out in their different settings, with the potential that the results in the four classrooms would help them better understand the inquiry learning and teaching process.

Like Trisha Kagey Boswell, Dorothy Simpson, and Chris Horne in earlier chapters, these teachers were conducting an inquiry on their inquiry teaching. And like Chris, in the course of their research, they changed their view of teaching: "As we learned more about inquiry teaching, we found ourselves also rethinking our own role in the classroom … In an inquiry classroom, the students ask the questions, and the teacher has to become a better listener and observer" (p. 121).

References

Dow, P. 1991. *Teacher education at the museum.* NSF 90-55474.

Dow, P. 1993. Teaching with objects: No fault learning. *Social Studies* 84(5): 230–231.

Kemmis, S., and R. McTaggert. 1988. *The action research planner,* 3rd ed. Victoria, Australia: Deakin University Press.

Learning About Motion: Fun for All!

Deborah L. Roberts

Deborah Roberts is a fifth-grade teacher in Phoenix, Arizona. At the time she wrote this chapter, she was a middle-school science teacher in a high-poverty suburban school in Maryland. An earlier version of this paper was presented at the University of Pennsylvania 21st Annual Ethnography in Education Research Forum in March 2000 and published in The Oregon Science Teacher. *Deborah begins her story by reflecting on an undergraduate physics course in which she learned how to ask questions and seek answers while using devices such as motion detectors and computers. Next she relates experiences when, as a beginning teacher, she brought her first-grade students to the physics lab so they could play with these devices. She also describes a seminar at her school during which she enticed several colleagues into learning about motion with these devices. She concludes with reflections upon engaging middle school students and student teachers in motion detector explorations.*

This is the seventh year in a row that I have used microcomputer-based laboratories with students and teachers after having taken a physics course as a prospective teacher. I will discuss four settings where this has taken place. The first was when I was taking the course; the second was when I brought my first-grade students to the physics lab; the third, when I co-taught the course to other teachers; and the fourth was the year with my sixth- and seventh-grade students. I will conclude with some reflections on the differences and commonalities of these experiences.

Physics and Prospective Teachers

One of the most valuable learning experiences I had was in an undergraduate physics class for future teachers. The reasons I value this experience are many. The instructor, John Layman, taught the class as inquiry (Layman et al. 1996). He designed the class as part of the Maryland Collaborative for Teacher Preparation (MCTP). MCTP faculty are reforming teacher education by redesigning college courses to model the way new teachers ought to teach mathematics and science. Dr. Layman's course embodied the instructional approach advocated in the National Science Education Standards, which state "inquiry into authentic questions generated from student experiences is the central strategy for teaching science" (NRC 1996, p. 31). He knew just how much information to give, which questions to ask, and when to let us struggle. He modeled what he taught.

Dr. Layman designed the physics course around microcomputer-based laboratories (MBL) (Krajcik and Layman 1993). At that time, "microcomputer" referred to a small version of regular computers which occupied an entire room. Today, the preferred term is "desktop computer." MBL typically refers to an instructional lab in which the students use a computer with some sort of probe attached to it so that the computer draws a graph as the student uses the probe. Students collect, graph, and then analyze data (Thornton 1987). The microcomputer gives students the opportunity to focus on analyzing data because the computer does the graph. This allows students to see the graph being plotted as they are conducting the experiment. Students can physically manipulate materials and the kind of information graphed, as well as the scales of both axes of the graph, and then instantly see the changes reflected on the graph (Linn 1991). They can make connections between manipulating the conditions and the real-time graph. Students associate the information obtained during the investigation through its representation on the graph. This application of technology is a powerful tool that helps students not only to better understand a graph and the information it contains but also to build science concepts (Krajcik and Layman 1993). MBLs also offer students an opportunity to learn using a variety of modalities. The students relate their experiences and observations with the graph being produced, and many are able to develop more sophisticated understandings of graphs (Brasell 1987; Makros and Tinker 1987; Settlage 1995).

In Dr. Layman's physics course, we started out with a motion detector but also used probes for temperature and force. Motion detectors are small boxes (probeware) that are connected to the microcomputers. When something moves in front of the box, the computer draws a graph to represent the motion—position versus time, velocity versus time, or acceleration versus time. After the motion is finished, one can shift among these graphs and compare them.

On the first day of class, Dr. Layman had the computers ready to go. He told us all we needed to do was have one person click on start and the other person stand about one meter away from the little box and see what happened. We were afraid to be very creative. We did not know what was expected. Dr. Layman walked around the room observing what we were doing and asking us to tell him about what we were observing and doing and why. We were watching the graph, which was a helpful tool for trying to understand what we were doing.

Teacher Research

When we came to a stopping point in the activity, Dr. Layman told us that our best resource in the room was our lab partner first and then other members of the class. He asked for one comment from each of us. We had to make a statement about what we were doing, and others were encouraged to comment on what we had said. This was very unnerving. As the class progressed, we all became very accustomed to doing this, and the questioning and arguing that ensued was very valuable in our continued learning.

We ended each class period with a list of statements and questions about what we believed had happened and what we wanted to know. Often our statements and questions changed from one class period to the next. Dr. Layman encouraged us to try and find the answer to our many questions, even if they were a little off the topic. We had not experienced this method of teaching in science classes in the past. As we became aware of the scientific concept, we were able to approach our learning in a different way and became a very cohesive, interdependent community of learners. Some students found the class frustrating, because we were not told that the right answer was *x* or that the right answer could be found on page 123 in the text. I found the class exhilarating and could not wait for the next session.

The motion experiments were my first formal experiences with the world of physics. I found these experiences to be wonderfully fulfilling times of learning. I felt constantly challenged and eager to learn more. Working with the technology of the MBL equipment was exciting and helped me to understand the concepts. I wanted my students to see that technology was a tool used by scientists, not just a reading program or a math game to play on the classroom computer. So when I finally had my own classroom, I wanted my students to have the experience I had.

Physics and First Graders

During my first year of teaching, I made arrangements to bring my first-grade students to Dr. Layman's physics course. This was a good opportunity for the prospective teachers to work with elementary students and a good opportunity for my students to not only have a good science learning experience but also to have a one-on-one experience with prospective teachers. This was important for two reasons. One, the first graders would have a broader understanding of what it means to be a teacher—that teachers have to go to class and do experiments and sometimes they do not know what the answers will be. And second, having taken this class, I felt it would have been valuable for us as preservice teachers to interact with young students in this way.

My first-grade students were extremely excited about going to the university to learn about science. In my classroom, from the first day, I tried to let my students know that each of them was a scientist. When we got to the physics classroom, they asked to be introduced as first-grade scientists to the class. The first graders were not nearly as inhibited as I remember being when I was first asked to experiment with the motion detector. They jumped right in and tried everything. It was not long before they were making connections between their body movements and the line on the graph on the computer. One little girl was pointing to the graph on the computer screen as she told her first-grade partner, "You did it! You made the line go up, and then it goes back down!"

The college students were amazed. My first graders figured out the connections among their movements and the line graphs sooner than the physics students did. "It took us forever to figure this out," the prospective teachers said. The first graders also had no qualms about volunteering information about their ideas on what was happening. They had no fears about saying someone else's idea was wrong when they experienced something differently. They were learning by challenging one another's ideas and testing their own. One group of students was trying to see if moving fast or slow made a difference in how the computer drew the line graph. The group developed a plan in which the first student would walk slowly and the second would walk quickly. The prospective teacher assisting them used a function of the graphing program to put one graph on top of the other so that they could compare them. They decided that the slow person needed to go even slower.

The first-grade students remained engaged for about 40 minutes before we asked them to stop and reflect on what they had been doing. These students were able to "develop descriptions, explanations, predictions, and models using evidence" (NRC 1996, p.145). They used their graphs as evidence when explaining what had happened. Dr. Layman observed, "When they were asked to describe their graphs by Debi, you could see that they were looking at their graph as they were generating their description. So they were literally reading their graphs and determining what to say from that."

Even the several students with limited English language skills could participate and understand because of the nature of the experiment, making connections between their activities and the graph they produced on the computer. All the students figured out enough about the motion detector to try to achieve specific results on the computer. Many of the students made mountains (lines that go up and then down) or volcanoes (mountains with a dip in the top). They chose the words to describe their activity. As Dr. Layman noted later about one of the groups of first graders, "I was impressed with that front group when I was on this side, and they were discussing with me and looking at the screen, at the sophistication of their terminology. I mean, it wasn't our formal terminology, but it was terminology that served them well in describing what was going on."

Teacher Research

Neither the first graders nor the college students left the activity with any doubts as to whether or not they were successful. They knew they were. Success is built into the inquiry method, because success is not based on right or wrong answers or how much content you absorbed in one class period. As encouraged by the National Science Education Standards (NRC 1996, p. 113), this course is designed to study a few physics concepts in depth as opposed to covering many topics.

The first graders left with a positive attitude about science and the nature of science. Their learning came from doing and thinking on their own rather than just hearing and then memorizing a set of science facts. They were self taught, benefiting from this hands-on class. Judging from the journal responses of the college students, they also left with a positive attitude about teaching and learning. All of the students—first grade and college—wanted to go back and do more. So did I. Unfortunately, the school year was almost at an end and going back was not a possibility. I considered this to have been a pilot project and did it again the next year with a new set of first graders and college students.

Physics and Experienced Teachers

After having the experiences of learning through the inquiry method and sharing those experiences with first graders, as described in the National Science Education Standards, Professional Development Standard A, that science teachers must "understand the nature of inquiry, its central role in science, and how to use the skills and processes of scientific inquiry" (NRC 1996, p. 59), I wanted to share this empowering kind of experience with my colleagues. Emily van Zee, who had been my science methods course instructor (van Zee 1998) and who also demonstrated this method of teaching, agreed to coteach a seminar meeting at my school.

This was exciting to me because most of the teacher inservices or courses offered through our county are taught by the lecture method. Although some encourage inquiry teaching, it is rare that one is taught using this method. It's hard for teachers who have never experienced inquiry to put it into practice after only hearing about it. So we developed a course as a model for the participating teachers. Professional Development Standard B states: Professional development "occurs in a variety of places where effective science teaching can be illustrated and modeled, permitting teachers to struggle with real situations and expand their knowledge and skills in appropriate contexts" and "use inquiry, reflection, interpretation of research, modeling, and guided practice to build understanding" (NRC 1996, p. 62).

Another uncommon component of the class was the use of technology. This is often discussed through lecture, but not often used. The content of the course was based on physical science. Specifically we focused on motion, distance, velocity, acceleration, and temperature. We began every class by rolling a ball down a ramp and asking the teachers to draw what they thought the graph of that motion would look like for distance, velocity, and acceleration versus time. The teachers were reluctant to do this initially and waited for a while to see what the others were going to draw before they risked making a mistake.

The next 30 to 45 minutes were spent inviting the teachers to move in front of the motion detector and try different things. The teachers, unfortunately, reminded me of myself and my fellow students in the physics course. They were hesitant to do anything—they did not even try to yell at the little box. Finally, one teacher got things started, and the others followed suit.

As they made graphs, they began to discuss them among themselves. They continually were dissatisfied with extraneous lines on the graph. The motion detector picked up the motion of their arms moving as they walked to and fro, and the lines of the graph were not perfectly and continually even. They tried all kinds of ways to walk without allowing their bodies any extra motion. One teacher took off her suit jacket in case that was getting in the way, and another teacher intentionally wore jeans to school for the next class, so that the motion detector would not pick up the swish of her skirt.

We provided the teachers with carts, but even these did not make satisfactory graphs for them. Instead of just pushing the cart off with their hands, they got metersticks to move the cart along, so their graphs would be smoother. Of course, they tried to walk at the same continual pace to ensure getting the kind of graph they wanted. They spent a lot of time problem solving and trying out different ways to achieve their desired results.

We would ask questions to try to guide their learning. The teachers eventually were able to understand the difference between distance, velocity, and acceleration. Later, we gave them graphs and asked them to try to reproduce them. To be able to do this they had to understand which physical property was used. They reproduced the graphs with fairly high accuracy.

Just as I had done in Dr. Layman's class, we asked the teachers to list questions they had at the end of the class and to summarize what they believed they had learned that day. At the beginning of the next class, we reviewed their questions and statements to help orient ourselves to the content again. They sometimes had given a lot of thought to a particular question or idea, and we encouraged them to try out their hypotheses through experimenting.

Observing the teacher's learning process was fascinating. They enjoyed using the technology of the MBLs because the graphs gave them immediate feedback. At times they would be only 10 seconds into a graph and decide that they needed to start over, because they wanted a different result. In addition to the discussion that we facilitated at the end of the class, the teachers seemed to be frequently involved in discussions of their own.

Teacher Research

Often, they were trying to relate what they were doing to other circumstances. A lively discussion ensued after one of the teachers made a connection between the motion detectors and the radar guns police use to measure speed. They not only activated prior knowledge but also made real-world connections.

At times, the teachers were very frustrated. They did not like not getting a direct answer. Often we would answer their questions with questions. By the middle of the course, they were relying more on each other and not looking to us as the sources of knowledge. They became good at articulating their problems or questions and proposing a possible solution. They were able to decide among themselves if the response they had come up with was feasible. Even if they left puzzled, they always appeared to be motivated to come back to the next class. "I am going to be the first one in front of that box next week—I know how to walk so we can get that graph," one teacher said. In between classes, there were many hallway discussions. There were many discussions about how to obtain the technology for our school, because what we were using was on loan from the university.

In the final piece of this project, the teachers took the equipment into their classrooms and gave their students the opportunity to experience the same things they had experienced. The teachers involved were third-, fourth-, and fifth-grade teachers who were all working with some aspect of graphing in their classroom and were able to easily fit this project into their current curriculum. None of the teachers were willing to use the technology on their own at first. All of them requested support and received support. Their students all had good experiences working with the technology, thanks to the help of a prospective teacher who was placed in my classroom and had taken the same physics course.

After using the MBLs in their classrooms, the teachers were eager to hear what had happened at the next class session. Part of their hesitation about using the equipment in their classrooms was due to the fact that they were not yet comfortable with their own understandings of motion. They were afraid their students might ask them to explain something they were not yet confident of. Despite this anxiety, they were excited by the responses of their students and their students' ability to begin to understand distance-versus-time graphs. Some teachers brought questions that they had from watching what the students did.

When the teachers got to temperature, they felt like they had a better understanding of the topic, and they had become more familiar with the technology. They did not hesitate this time to bring the technology into the classroom and give the students the opportunity to experiment. One teacher kept the equipment in her classroom for almost a month. She was very excited that her students were making mathematical as well as science connections.

All of the teachers were disappointed that there was not going to be another class the following semester. They had all enjoyed the class and the experience in inquiry learning and teaching. They felt as if they were continuing the learning that is essential for teachers. They stumbled, wrestled, and pondered while realizing that failure is a natural part of developing new skills and understanding (NRC 1996, p. 69). We were able to provide a situation that "involved teachers in actively investigating phenomena that can be studied scientifically, interpreting results, and making sense of findings consistent with currently accepted scientific understandings" (ibid.). And we all enjoyed doing it!

Physics and Middle School Students

In my fourth year of teaching, I felt that the MBL was too good to give up. Fortunately, I still had that connection with the university, and was fortunate enough to have four MBL setups in my classroom. I was teaching sixth- and seventh-grade math, and graphing is a part of both grade-level curricula. I had been fortunate to have a group of prospective teachers come into my classroom each semester to do a reflective research project. Those selected to come to my class had experienced the physics course for prospective elementary teachers. So, it is not hard to guess what the context for their research project was.

A group of four prospective teachers came to my classroom in the fall to work with a seventh-grade class, and a different group came to work with a sixth-grade class. They were interested in seeing what happened when the sixth and seventh graders had their first experience with the motion detectors. We met before the lesson so that they could plan what their research question would be for the experience and how they would execute the lesson in a way that would provide them with insight on their research question. Next, they came and observed the class for one period to get a feel for the kids and the classroom environment. Finally, they came and tried out their lesson with the sixth and seventh graders.

I never fail to be amazed at what actually happens when young people interact with the MBL technology. The sixth and seventh graders were not given very specific directions, only to try to find out what the little box connected to the computer was. Both groups of students began by screaming and yelling at the motion detector. They clapped their hands, they spoke to it, and they turned it upside down. They spent a good amount of time just crowded around it. They did not appear to be shy or inhibited about trying to figure this out. When screaming and yelling didn't work, they went to jumping. Jumping actually caused something to happen on the graph. This led to a fairly rapid transition to walking or running in front of the motion detector. They were often so excited that they did not realize at first that it was much better if only one person at a time moved in front of the device.

I asked each group of students to write a short summary of what they had learned after experimenting with the MBL. Both groups of students seemed to understand the function of the device and directionality of motion. The following list of comments demonstrates some of their understandings.

Defining the Device

Seventh-grade female—On Tuesday we had to figure out how to use motion devices. A motion device is a device that you connect to your computer, and the further you walk away from it, the line on the computer increase. That means if you walk closer to the line, it will decrease. The motion device only picks up what is in front of it. A motion device measures distance and time of motions.

Seventh-grade male—We talked about a whole bunch of things, but the one that got us thinking was when we moved by the box. The graph on the computer showed a line on how we moved.

Sixth-grade female—I learned about motion detectors and what they do. It detects how far away something is in seconds.

Sixth-grade male—I learned what it is—that it measures how far you are away and how many seconds you did that.

Seventh-grade female—What I am going to tell you is what I learned about what a motion detector is. A motion detector is like a small machine that measures how far your distance is in how many seconds.

Directionality of Motion

Seventh-grade female—If you get away from it, the graph line goes up. If you go close, the graph line goes down.

Sixth-grade male—You make the line go up by moving back, and if you want it to go down, you have to move (to the) front.

Sixth-grade female—I have learned that, when you move back, the line in the computer screen goes higher up, and, when you come close, the line goes down.

Rate of Speed

Sixth-grade female—You do not have very much time if you are trying to make a graph that looks like this: [many squiggles]. You have to go fast.

Sixth-grade female—If you are moving fast, the line zigzags a lot.

Sixth-grade female—If you go slow, the lines look like low mountains.

Seventh-grade grade male—The faster you move, the straighter it [the line] goes up.

Sixth-grade male—I also learned that if you move backwards or forwards and change your pace, it will make a curve on the graph.

It seems that there was definitely some preliminary understanding that occurred, with some students beginning to articulate ideas not only about time versus distance but velocity and acceleration as well. My experiences have led me to see the MBL equipment as a powerful tool in enhancing understanding of physics and mathematics. The class I originally took as an undergraduate was also a powerful tool in learning to teach (and learn) through inquiry. The instruction that I received gave me the model that I strive to achieve in my own classroom. I believe it has had an effect on the prospective teachers who came to my classroom also.

Methods Students and Student Teachers

I have worked with both methods students and student teachers over the past three years. (Methods students are enrolled in courses on methods of teaching science, mathematics, social studies, language arts, and reading in the semester before they student teach.) Many of these students had the same physics class and experiences similar to the one I had. Some did not. In reflecting on these two groups of preservice teachers, I have noticed some differences. The students who took the physics course appeared to have a positive attitude toward science and seemed to exhibit a certain confidence about being able to learn and teach physics. One of the benefits gained from the class is a deep conceptual understanding of the topics covered. As a student, you learn to have the confidence to take risks and to feel you are capable of learning science.

The prospective teachers from physics also seemed to feel fairly confident about allowing the students to discover science ideas. They let them "mess around," as one student put it, until they figured it out. They believed that the students were capable of coming to some understanding. They were more comfortable in facilitating learning rather than transmitting learning, because they, too, had had the experience of having their learning guided instead of given.

These prospective teachers encouraged student discussion, ideas, questions, and reflections. They helped the students articulate their thoughts and ideas. They were not intimidated by the possibility of not having an answer, because they saw their physics professor excited by questions they had for which he did not have an immediate answer.

They knew that sometimes learning does not fit the time constraints of the classroom, and that, if they needed to continue the next day, it was OK. The big idea did not have to be told in the summary of the lesson. Instead, having the students summarize what they had learned so far was enough.

Another strategy I noticed they used was that of activating prior knowledge. They started with an activity that helped students activate what they already knew and tried to help them apply it to the new situation. They were becoming good listeners and solicited information from students through the use of questioning and sometimes through rephrasing student statements.

I am curious about whether or not this would continue to hold true should I test my hypothesis on a larger scale and through observations of others. For the 20 or so methods students with whom I have worked and the student teachers with whom I have worked closely, as well as peers who came through the same education program I went through, there seem to be some notable differences. Those of us who took the physics course definitely share one characteristic—we are extremely grateful for having had the experience and would like everyone else to have it too.

Reflecting

For my personal learning experience in this class, the physics course had modeled what the National Science Education Standards define as abilities necessary to do scientific inquiry—"students should experience science in a form that engages them in the active construction of ideas and explanations and enhances their opportunities to develop the abilities of doing science" (NRC 1996, p.121). During their experience in the college setting, the first graders had been able to "use the data to construct a reasonable explanation … emphasizing the students' thinking as they use data to formulate explanations … students should learn what constitutes evidence and judge the merits or strength of the data and information that will be used to make explanations" (NRC 1996, p. 122). I think this is true of the sixth- and seventh-graders and the experienced teachers, even though the experienced teachers were slightly more inhibited and initially frustrated by the philosophy of teaching being implemented.

These experiences demonstrate to me what has been documented about computer-based instruction: using computers in the classroom usually improves student achievement and is cost effective. (Kulik and Kulik 1991; Bialo and Silvin 1991). Collins's work (1991) showed that "when technology was introduced into the classroom, teaching styles changed from whole-class to small groups, lectures were replaced with coaching." Maybe this is part of the reason the prospective teachers, methods students, and student teachers who have taken the physics course are different from those who have not.

Reflections

Here, we shift our focus. Although this chapter contains questioning, evidence collection, sense making, and sharing, its importance is in illuminating the process by which a person, whether a student or a teacher, first feels the exhilaration of learning through inquiry. Using herself as an example, Deborah describes her feelings as she began the physics class where she first felt this. She takes us through the stages of her experience: "We were afraid to be very creative. We did not know what was expected." Later in the first class, "[Dr. Layman] asked for one comment from each of us. This was a very unnerving experience.... As the class progressed, we all became very accustomed to doing this, and the questioning and arguing that ensued was very valuable in our continued learning." Finally, " ... we were able to approach our learning in a different way, and became a very cohesive, interdependent community of learners" (pp. 125–126).

Deborah describes bringing this experience to her first-grade class, to other teachers, to middle school students, and to preservice teachers. The network of people involved in her sharing of this crucial learning experience covered many students and teachers, including her student teacher, Trisha Kagey Boswell (Chapter 3), and a colleague at another school, Kathleen Dillon Hogan, who went on to use motion detectors with her students as described in Chapter 1. Each group experienced the same pleasure at learning this way: "Neither the first graders nor the college students left the activity with any doubts as to whether or not they were successful. They knew they were. Success is built into the inquiry method ... " (pp. 127–128).

Deborah, and all of us who have contributed to this collection of teacher research, value inquiry for its power to allow us to answer our own questions about teaching and learning through collecting evidence, making sense of the evidence, and sharing with colleagues.

References

Bialo, E. and J. Silvin. 1991. Effectiveness of microcomputers in schools: Effects on student achievement. *Emergency Librarian* 19 (1): 54–56.

Brasell, H. 1987. The effect of real-time laboratory graphing on learning graphic representations of distance and velocity. *Journal of Research in Science Teaching* 24(4): 385–395.

Collins, 1991. "Technology Tools for Transforming Teaching/Learning" from the Department of Education Publications website: *www.ed.gov/pubs/TeachersGuide/pt21.html.* (not retrievable July 29, 2006)

Krajcik, J. S., and J. W. Layman. 1993. Micro-based laboratories in the science classroom. *National Association for Research on Science Teaching Newsletter* 31: 3–6.

Kulik, J., and C. Kulik. 1991. Effectiveness of computer-based instruction: An updated analysis. *Computers in Human Behavior* 7(1–2): 75–94.

Layman, J. W., G. Ochoa, and H. Heikkinen. 1996. *Inquiry and learning: Realizing science standards in the classroom.* New York: College Entrance Examination Board.

Linn, M. C. 1991. The computer as learning partner: Can computers teach science? In *This year in school science 1991: Technology for teaching and learning,* eds. L. Roberts, K. Sheingold, and S. Malcolm. Washington, DC: American Association for the Advancement of Science.

Makros, J. R., and R. F. Tinker. 1987. The impact of microcomputer-based labs on children's ability to interpret graphs. *Journal of Research in Science Teaching* 24: 369–383.

National Research Council (NRC). 1996. *National Science Education Standards*. Washington, DC: National Academy Press.

Roberts, D. L. 2004. Learning about motion: Fun for all! *The Oregon Science Teacher* 46 (2): 21–29.

Settlage, J. 1995. Children's conceptions of light in the context of a technology-based curriculum. *Science Education* 79: 535–553.

Thornton, R. 1987. Tools for scientific thinking—Microcomputer-based laboratories for physics teaching. *Physics Education* 22(4): 230–238.

van Zee, E. H. 1998. Preparing teachers as researchers in courses on methods of teaching science. *Journal of Research in Science Teaching* 35: 791–809.

Reflections on Fostering Teacher Inquiries Into Science Learning and Teaching

Emily Hanke van Zee

Emily van Zee is an associate professor of science education at Oregon State University and co-organizer of Teacher Researcher Day at National Science Teachers Association (NSTA) national conferences. She has been a middle school science teacher, scout leader, physics instructor, and science teacher educator. While a faculty member at the University of Maryland, College Park, she initiated and facilitated the Science Inquiry Group with graduates of her courses and their colleagues. As a university professor, Emily found that collaborating with K–12 teachers prompted major shifts in her roles as a teacher and as a researcher. Both she and the teachers faced challenges in negotiating new perspectives on their relative status, modes of discourse during meetings, time required for collaboration, and ways to communicate the knowledge generated. In this chapter, she reflects upon these challenges and the personal history that underlies her commitment and approaches to fostering teacher research.

How do I view my experiences in fostering teachers' inquiries into science teaching and learning over many years in many contexts? Below I articulate a shift in roles that these efforts required, challenges that the teachers and I encountered, and the experiences that underlie my particular approaches to facilitating collaborative inquiries. I close with some thoughts about the process of researching while teaching.

Shifts in Roles

Fostering teacher research has shifted my roles as a university faculty member in both teaching and research. An emphasis on collaboration has increased in the ways I have taught my courses (van Zee 1998b, 2005a; Valli et al. 2006) and have worked with groups of practicing teacher researchers (van Zee 1998a, van Zee et al. 2003).

As a traditional instructor in a large lecture course, I used to select the topics to be studied, decide upon required readings, specify assignments, lecture on points that seemed important to me, make and administer tests, and calculate grades based on the students' performance on the midterm and final examinations. In my current courses, however, I view myself as a facilitator rather than instructor. Instead of selecting specific topics, I plan the terrain to be explored. Now I invite students to focus on the readings that seem most interesting to them from an array that I suggest and to which they can contribute. My assignments describe the boundaries of both individual and group endeavors and engage students in examining issues they formulate within the contexts I establish. My assessments are ongoing, both of the processes of learning in class and the products produced. These shifts in roles are due not only to a change in the number of students (from about 100 to 30 or fewer) and topic (from statistics to science education) but also to growth in my understanding about ways to promote learning.

In traditional approaches to educational research, university faculty direct projects by formulating the questions examined, designing the studies, collecting and analyzing data, and communicating results. Participating teachers usually are anonymous subjects who may or may not be aware of the intent of the studies nor informed of the findings. In my collaborative approach, however, I view myself as an organizer rather than director of research. My roles include creating a vision to guide research, organizing events to promote progress, seeking resources to sustain our collaboration, consulting and editing as needed, and offering encouragement and support as teachers begin participating along the spectrum of deciding what issues to explore, designing their studies, collecting and interpreting their data, presenting findings at conferences, building documentary websites, and submitting papers for publication. I discuss these roles below.

Creating a vision to guide research. What does it mean to do research? Many people associate educational research only with quantitative studies, in which a university researcher designs an intervention to improve instruction, collects data from treatment and control groups, and uses statistics to analyze differences in outcomes. From my perspective, research activities span a spectrum (see Table 1 of the Preface) that also includes briefly noticing and wondering about something in the midst of teaching. A next step might be keeping a record of such moments: What were the particulars that prompted the noticing and wondering? Is there a pattern in these moments? How would one go about finding out what makes these moments happen?

Teacher *Research*

Many graduate programs include courses in action research with a focus on identifying problems and seeking solutions through careful observation and trial of alternatives. However, I have a bias toward understanding success. When I meet with a group of teachers interested in inquiring into their own teaching practices, I ask "What are you curious about that's happening in your classroom? What is going well for you and your students? Why? How can you document those successes and share your findings to help others?" I prefer to emphasize a teacher's passion rather than troubleshoot whatever seems to be causing pain.

In addition to focusing upon positives, I encourage teachers to gather a wide variety of data. For me, *data* refers to more than scores on tests or numbers circled on surveys. I encourage teachers to regard almost everything as potential data—what students say and do as recorded on videotape; what students draw and write for assignments, in book margins, or even notes dropped on the floor; what the teachers write themselves in lesson plans, anecdotal records, journals; what they and colleagues write in e-mail messages; whatever artifacts seem relevant—all of these can contribute to evidence that teachers consider in trying to make sense of issues they have formulated. I also do the work of going through an Institutional Review Board process under the umbrella of my research program on science learning and teaching so that teachers with whom I collaborate have official consent forms to use in undertaking their studies.

Reporting on research also can take many forms. For me, a poem can be appropriate (See "Jonathan" by Ellen Franz in Chapter 5). I encourage teachers to write narratives rather than formal reports, grounded in data such as a transcript of a conversation or copies of student written work. Such detailed accounts of what happened in particular instances of science learning can help others envision effective approaches to science teaching. The chapters in this volume, for example, are intended as examples of the inquiry-based instruction recommended in *National Science Education Standards* (NRC 1996). Documentary websites, such as co-editor Claire Bove's (*http://feelingathome.org*), also provide an effective way to represent the complexity of science learning and teaching.

Organizing events to promote progress. Any teacher can undertake research in any setting. It helps, though, to have colleagues with whom to discuss what one is doing and thinking. My belief is that students' opportunities to learn will improve as teachers in a school seek to understand what is working well for their students and how they can widen and deepen those successes. But just finding a time and place to meet can be a challenge. Having an outsider come to the school may provide an incentive to overcoming the many obstacles to meeting regularly.

When facilitating a teacher inquiry group informally at a school or formally in a university course, I open the first meeting with a conversation about what it means to do research. Often some members of the group have participated in traditional projects where the university person was in charge, where "teacher" and "researcher" were different people with distinctly different roles. The agenda for this first meeting is to open discussion of my alternative vision of research, one in which "teaching" and "researching" can be undertaken in the same moment by the same person.

Looking at examples of teacher research is a good way to start, in articles (Iwasyk 1997; Roberts 1999; Simpson 1997) and books (Doris 1991; Gallas 1995; Pearce 1999). What questions did these teachers ask, and how did they go about seeking answers? After discussing such examples of teacher research, I invite participants to begin thinking about questions such as "What are you curious about your own students' learning?" "How could you explore that issue?"

We also look at abstracts written by participants in earlier seminars. An abstract includes a title, a sentence or two that defines the issue being examined, and another sentence or two that describes data sources that will be collected and interpreted. For example, this from Chapter 3:

Fourth-Grade Scientists Investigate Electric Circuits
Trisha Kagey Boswell
As a first-year teacher, I am curious about how I can model an authentic scientific inquiry experience with my fourth-grade students. We began our exploration of electric circuits with questions that the students asked. Cooperative groups are developing hypotheses and designing investigations to answer their questions. Students will communicate their results at a "Scientists' Conference." In this case study, I am monitoring how students perceive themselves as scientists as they figure things out. Data sources include the student displays, their reflections in their journals, and taped discussions.

I encourage participants to write such abstracts right there in this first meeting. Acknowledging that the focus of their research likely will change, I ask each to think over our earlier discussion about what interests them in their own settings and to define an issue that seems important, describe a way to explore this issue, and create a tentative title. Leaving the meeting with a particular plan in mind can provide a sense of direction for participants uncomfortable with amorphous tasks (or a sense of panic for those uncomfortable with such immediate specificity).

Another way to get started is to ask participants to notice instances of science learning in progress during the coming week, to describe one of these in detail, and then to step back and ponder, "What were the factors that fostered this learning?" This is the ongoing assignment for journal writing in my courses (van Zee and Roberts 2001; van Zee 2005a) and can seem useful to participants in informal groups as well. Out of a series of such journals may emerge a focus that becomes the participant's research question.

Subsequent meetings begin with a round robin. What has each participant been noticing and wondering since we last met? What is each participant considering now for a research question? Later, what progress has each participant made in designing ways to answer the question? In collecting data? Still later, what progress has each participant made in interpreting data? In writing? We hear from everybody at the beginning of a session, at least briefly, before focusing upon the main event. I think people make progress—even if only a little—when they know they'll have to report—even if briefly—to the group.

Usually the main event for a session involves one of the participants engaging the others in thinking with them about what question(s) to ask, what data to gather, how to interpret some example data, or how to express better the findings, depending upon where the participant is in the research process. Preparing to do this prompts major progress. However, the others also make progress as they make connections to and sometimes discuss their own concerns within their colleague's context. One organizational structure that worked well for a major project was to have two "main events" in which two participants showed and discussed a video and/or their students' work, each for 45 minutes, back to back. My usual practice with teachers inquiry groups was to open with a general "how are things going" conversation while people gathered, then have one person facilitate an in-depth discussion of his or her students' learning for an hour or so, and then close with a general conversation about people's plans. In this program, however, we opened with a very brief period to get organized (4:30–4:45), then one teacher facilitated a conversation about his or her students' learning (4:45–5:30), followed by another teacher (5:30–6:15), and we ended with a very brief closing (6:15–6:30).

A research festival concludes a course or, for an informal seminar, an agreed-upon time span. The participants prepare posters and papers reporting on their projects, with time for "writers' workshops" for mutual assistance in preparation for this event. They present their findings to one another and sometimes to others at school staff meetings or in other courses. These in-house research festivals are good preparation for more formal settings. Some participants choose to go on to present at conferences and to submit their papers for publication.

Seeking resources to sustain collaboration. As a university faculty member, my responsibilities include seeking funding from government agencies and private foundations. Traditionally, grants have supported a faculty member's research—to buy equipment the researcher uses, to provide stipends as an incentive for subjects to participate, to pay for staff to assist the researcher in data collection and analysis, and to cover travel costs for the researcher to present at conferences. I was fortunate to obtain funding from the Spencer Foundation's program for practitioner research so that I could buy equipment for participating teachers to use, provide stipends to support some of the time and effort they were putting into collecting and analyzing their own data, and to cover their travel costs to present at conferences. Writing proposals is not among the expectations for teachers, nor do they typically have access to mentors experienced in seeking funding. Investing the time and effort necessary to garner resources—cameras, tapes, books, funding for substitutes, support for travel—seems to me to be essential for university faculty members committed to fostering teacher research.

Consulting and editing as needed. Blocking out sufficient time to prepare papers for publication is an expected part of my workday. Teachers who choose to write, however, are squeezing in moments during the day and spending late evenings and weekends to articulate their questions and findings. My advice has been to write in ways that colleagues can understand and value, to write for other members of one's grade-level team, for the beginning teacher down the hall, for another teacher who can learn from reading and thinking about whatever issue is being examined. I suggest finding a journal for teachers that seems appropriate for the topic, such as one of the National Science Teachers Association journals, and using the directions for authors to guide the writing process. My emphasis has been on writing in engaging ways that present the issues they have been exploring and include evidence of their students' learning. Sometimes I suggest a relevant research article to read but do not emphasize extensive literature reviews. It seems more important to me that teachers use their limited time available in articulating well their own findings for their immediate audiences. As participants bring their studies to a close for a course or informal seminar, I encourage them to assist one another by reading and commenting during a series of writers' workshops or e-mail exchanges. Their teaching colleagues represent their best sources of feedback, but I try to respond promptly to e-mails when queried and to offer constructive comments on papers submitted for course projects.

Offering encouragement and support. Perhaps the most important role of a university faculty member in fostering teacher research is what I think of as cheerleading, offering a consistently positive voice of encouragement to those attempting something they may have never done before, that differs from expectations, and that may seem audacious to even attempt. I also have found that this is a mutual process, that the teachers with whom I collaborate have formed a wonderful support group for me as I have progressed through the university tenure and promotion process.

Challenges

These collaborative roles have created some challenges. One issue is status. My status as a university professor seems to be intimidating initially for some of the experienced teachers who have joined our enterprises. Like the students in my courses, they seem to expect me to tell them what to do and to make judgments about how well they are performing. When they receive continuing professional development credit for participating in a seminar, I retain officially the force of that status: I can choose to sign or not to sign the form that informs their county of their participation. Similarly, no matter how collaborative an environment I try to create in my courses, at the end of the term I must assign grades that reflect my assessment of the students' progress.

A second issue concerns the discourse practices at our meetings and in class. To what extent should I control, guide, or simply observe the talk? At our Science Inquiry Group meetings, I initially tried to direct the conversation toward my own agenda. Eventually I chose simply to enjoy the teachers' stories and let them move themselves toward more focused discussions. I face a similar issue in class. If I ask students to plan and facilitate group discussions, what role remains for me to play when vigorous and thoughtful conversations consistently emerge without my direct input?

A third issue concerns the quality of the products. We have wonderful and insightful discussions, but the teachers have limited time to write and little experience in producing research reports. They seem to enjoy formulating issues to examine, collecting relevant data, sharing and interpreting these data with their colleagues, but the next step of writing is difficult. For formal courses taught at the university, participants expect to and do write papers; for informal groups meeting at schools, particularly if no credit of any kind is involved, the experiences can be wonderful but the expectations on both sides are more diffuse.

A fourth issue concerns time management. Although school-based research groups make sense because the teachers can collaborate together between meetings and do not have to travel or park to get to the meetings, multiple meetings at different sites are more time intensive for me. When participants are from different schools, as often is the case when I continue to meet with graduates of our program, holding the meetings at a central location— a participant's classroom, a public library—makes sense but still requires travel time for us all.

A cluster of issues revolves around the research itself. Teachers who videotape their classes and show the tapes to others are taking risks. The viewers may choose to criticize and condemn whatever captures their attention rather than to appreciate the particular issue that is the teacher's focus. Conducting research and presenting at conferences can change the way a teacher is viewed by colleagues and administrators, sometimes in positive ways but also sometimes negative. Research that focuses on problems can create intense stresses by making these public. That is one reason I have advocated identifying positive practices and trying to understand and disseminate these.

Experiences Facilitating Collaborative Inquiry

How did I learn what I have come to know about forming and facilitating collaborative inquiry groups? Some readers also may be curious about how the authors of these chapters were involved in the experiences that underlie what I do. Below I reflect upon what happened in a series of settings: my middle school science classroom, free-choice learning activities, physics courses for teachers, a high school physics research site, studies of questioning during conversations about science, education courses and research seminars, science education courses and Science Inquiry Group seminars, a physics seminar, a Science and Technology Inquiry Group seminar, Student Inquiry in Physical Science seminars, the Carnegie Academy for the Scholarship of Teaching Learning, Looking at Data seminars, collaborative inquiries at national meetings, and Teacher Researcher Day at National Science Teachers Association national conferences.

Middle School Science Classroom. As a middle school science teacher, I taught the way I had been taught and perceived myself as being expected to teach. When I first entered my classroom, the desks were lined up in straight rows, and they stayed that way. It never occurred to me to move the desks together so my students could work and converse in small groups. The school had no laboratory space and little equipment. I expected my students to listen to me or to work quietly by themselves unless we were having a whole-group discussion. The discussions were more like recitations than shared thinking as individual students responded to questions I had asked. The concept of collaborative inquiry was absent from my repertoire.

Free-Choice Learning Activities. As a parent volunteer in elementary schools, I offered science experiences that were more open-ended than usual. During these years at home, I also enjoyed planning and leading scout activities that focused on science rather than crafts. These provided many opportunities for me to enjoy listening to children thinking creatively and productively with one another in science contexts.

Physics Courses for Teachers. When I returned to work, I experienced very different formal ways of teaching as a staff member for physics courses for teachers at the University of Washington (McDermott 1990, 1996). These courses met entirely in a laboratory, with small groups of four working at tables and talking together as they explored various physical phenomena. Here I learned to move from group to group, to listen closely to what was being said, and to make a pertinent comment or ask a question designed to move the thinking forward. As one of the other staff members said to me after I had spent a long time explaining something to one of the students, "This is the weirdest physics course I have ever seen, but it works; it's really important that you don't tell answers. Be sure that the student is holding the pencil and answer a question with a question." Eventually, as lead instructor for many of these courses, I became responsible for taking new staff members aside and trying to coach these very different ways of teaching and learning. Whole-group discussions occurred in these courses, but only after the small groups had had extensive experience with particular phenomena. The purpose was to report what the small groups had observed and to make sense of these various observations. My role was to facilitate coming to agreement about what had been seen and what one could infer from these observations, a very different process from the recitations I had conducted in my middle school classroom.

High School Physics Research Site. My initial model for collaborative inquiry among practicing teachers was a research group established by a high school physics teacher, Jim Minstrell (1989, 2001) (see Foreword). He obtained grants that paid for two mathematics colleagues—Dorothy Simpson and Virginia Stimpson—to teach some of his classes so that he could devote part of the day to thinking about, exploring, and writing about his students' learning. As he coached these experienced math teachers in teaching physics, the three formed an inspiring learning community that I was privileged to join as a university researcher, learning from them as they learned from one another (see Dorothy Simpson's study of collaborative dialogue in Chapter 9). Jim emphasized identifying useful intuitions on which students could build to enlarge their areas of physics competence. This is the origin of my orientation toward expanding successes rather than troubleshooting problems in the classroom. My postdoctoral research focused narrowly upon ways Jim used questioning to guide student thinking (van Zee and Minstrell 1997a, b) but my experiences here formed a broad expectation: that teachers can and should generate knowledge, that is, that knowledge can and should flow from schools to universities as well as the reverse.

Studies of Questioning During Conversations About Science. With support from the National Science Foundation, I continued my studies of questioning during conversations about science with a group of teachers who taught at many different schools (van Zee et al. 2001). However, all had participated in the physics programs for teachers at the University of Washington and engaged their students in inquiries into physical phenomena. I collaborated with these teachers individually by videotaping in their classrooms, selecting and transcribing discussions I found interesting, writing interpretations from my perspective of what was happening, revising according to their feedback, and presenting findings with them as coauthors at conferences. After I moved, however, several chose to continue this work by videotaping themselves, selecting, transcribing, and writing interpretations of discussions they found interesting, and presenting as first or sole authors at conferences where I had submitted group proposals (Iwasyk 1997; Kurose 2000; Simpson 1997; Wild 2000). This shifted my role from a university researcher collaborating with teachers to further *my* research to collaborating with teachers to facilitate *their* research. We met as a group occasionally when I returned to Seattle for visits. These were my first experiences in facilitating conversations among teachers who were working on their own projects individually. We had a shared history and commitment to inquiry so they were comfortable expressing clearly to me, that, although important, questioning was only one of many relevant issues they were interested in exploring. In order to use my grant's resources for trips to conferences, however, they had to include a focus on questioning in their studies.

Education Courses and Research Seminars. As the SESAME (Search for Excellence in Science and Mathematics Education) Lecturer at the University of California at Berkeley, I joined an effort just getting under way to educate future mathematics and science teachers in the same courses as future educational researchers (Schoenfeld et al. 1999). Here I participated in and taught courses where discussion was expected and encouraged, where the focus was on what one thinks and why one thinks that and how that relates to what others think, both those in the room and those whose views were expressed in the readings. Some of the readings were by faculty who included experienced teachers as research partners (diSessa et al. 1991). I also went to the weekly meetings of several research groups and formed a research group of my own that included both prospective teachers such as coeditor Claire Bove and prospective researchers. Participants in these research groups took turns presenting and discussing data such as video clips of students in action or copies of students' writings and drawings. The faculty sponsoring the research groups were present and contributed to the thinking, but the responsibility for planning and facilitating group meetings lay with the graduate students, both those who were preparing to be teachers and those preparing to be educational researchers. These experiences formed my model of how to foster research by sponsoring collaborative meetings in which the participants plan and facilitate the discussions. Here also I first submitted a group proposal for a session at a professional conference: Eight of us presented individual studies together at the International Conference for Teacher Research that happened to be meeting at a nearby university.

Science Education Courses and Science Inquiry Group Seminars. As an assistant professor at the University of Maryland, I used "teacher as researcher" as the metaphor underlying the design of my courses on methods of teaching science in elementary and middle school (van Zee 1998b; 2005a). To find out what, if anything, was useful in these courses, I invited graduates to join me in forming a Science Inquiry Group (SING) so that I could learn from their experiences as beginning teachers. Diantha Lay (Chapter 12) and Deborah Roberts (Chapter 13) were founding members of this group. We met monthly after school in one of the participants' classrooms, along with several experienced teachers who had become interested in our enterprises. With a grant from the Spencer Foundation, I was able to provide cameras, tape recorders, tapes, and books (such as Doris 1991; Gallas 1995; Hubbard and Power 1993, 1999; Pearce 1999; Saul et al. 2000; White and Gunstone 1992) to support the SING teachers' learning and inquiries. I had written the proposal so that participants would not be constrained to investigate only questioning; these teachers examined a wide variety of issues in the context of their science-teaching practices.

Each semester, we put on our own Research Festival, at which the SING teachers presented their findings to the prospective teachers in my current course. Eventually, they also mentored small groups of my students in designing and conducting pilot studies of science learning and teaching in the SING teachers' classrooms (van Zee et al. 2003). Although the process was a logistics nightmare, these were truly collaborative inquiries, with prospective teachers, beginning teachers, and experienced teachers all contributing. This process culminated in a second Research Festival in which my students presented their findings to the SING teachers. At one point, I was facilitating science inquiry groups in three counties with graduates of my course who had enjoyed this process of learning to do research as they learned to teach. Our home-grown research festivals were good practice for those interested in going to conferences. The grant paid registration and travel expenses for SING teachers to present their studies at National Science Teachers Association conferences, the Ethnography in Education Research Forum at the University of Pennsylvania, annual meetings of the National Association for Research in Science Teaching and the American Educational Research Association, and several International Conferences for Teacher Research.

Physics Seminar. One of the graduates of my course, Deborah Roberts, interested several colleagues in meeting every other week after school for a seminar that we cotaught. I arranged to offer this for professional development credit through the state department of education. She invited the teachers to play with motion detectors, devices that send signals to a computer which then displays a line graph that represents one's motion while one is moving (*http://elementary.vernier.com*). She had learned to interpret motion graphs with these devices in an undergraduate physics course. Both her physics instructor, Professor John Layman, and I had been astonished when she brought her first-grade students to visit the physics course and the children had quickly learned how to "read" the line graphs representing their own motions. She wanted teachers at her school to learn how to use these engaging devices with their students, most of whom came from low-income and immigrant families. These experienced teachers were assisted by a prospective teacher, Trisha Kagey Boswell, also a graduate of the physics course, who had been placed in Deborah's classroom while enrolled in education courses, including my course on methods of teaching science in elementary and middle school. This experience formed my model for high-quality professional development—an ongoing seminar with teachers across grade levels in the same school that utilizes technology to enhance subject matter knowledge; applies directly in the classrooms; and stimulates discussions about student learning. Furthermore, knowledge flows not only to the school from the university graduates as well as faculty but also from the school to the university through the teachers' experiences and written reflections.

Science and Technology Inquiry Group Seminar. Another graduate of my course, Kathleen Hogan, participated in a professional development seminar at her school, which was acquiring state-of-the art technology through a state program. I invited participants to formulate questions about their emerging use of technology, to collect data in their own classrooms, and to develop case studies that could communicate to their colleagues and others the successes they were experiencing as they integrated technology into their instructional programs. All of us were risking undertaking something about which we felt vulnerable and unprepared. Initially many of the teachers seemed apprehensive about viewing themselves as researchers. Some had participated in university-based projects in which the roles of teacher and researcher had been clearly separated. I was apprehensive about offering a technology-based seminar because I knew little about using SMARTboards and sets of laptop computers in classroom settings. We began by meeting several times during the fall to plan the spring seminar: What would be helpful as they began to try to use the new technologies that were going to be arriving soon? How often would they want to meet? Where? When? For what purpose? These planning sessions enabled us to begin spring semester with a schedule of dates, times, goals, and activities that the teachers had collaborated in articulating. I learned an enormous amount from these teachers as they developed their case studies with examples of student work and discussions of issues they encountered in using various technologies.

All of the teachers presented their findings to their colleagues at a research festival at their school. Some posted materials on websites, presented their case studies at two local conferences for teacher researchers, and submitted refined versions for publication in journals for teachers.

Student Inquiry in Physical Science (SIPS) Seminars. With support from the National Science Foundation, David Hammer and I collaborated with about 15 elementary and middle school teachers in developing case studies of student inquiries in physical science (Hammer and van Zee 2006). Mary Bell, Kathleen Hogan, Christopher Horne, Trisha Kagey Boswell, and Deborah Roberts were participants in this project. During the summers, David engaged the participants in learning physics through discussion of scenarios based in everyday contexts. He wanted participants to "shop for ideas" based on their everyday experiences, to try these ideas out to see what they might imply, and to learn to recognize and reconcile conflicting accounts. In contrast to many inquiry-based programs that begin by engaging students in exploring physical phenonema, he began with extended discussions in which participants proposed, justified, and contemplated various responses. Eventually participants played with phenomena but not until they had articulated issues to guide these explorations. During the academic years, the participants came to the university every other week after school for two hours to meet with staff members in small groups. During the first hour, one participant in each group presented a "snippet" for discussion such as a video clip of a conversation about science or a set of student papers. During the second hour, another participant did the same. These were intense experiences in which all of us learned from one another. Each semester, the participants wrote up their interpretations of one of their snippets as a case study, and during the summers they refined the best of these into final versions. They were assisted by staff members who videotaped in their classrooms, transcribed portions the teachers indicated as important, and discussed with great interest nuances of the students' ideas. Here the emphasis was on the elementary and middle school students' reasoning rather than on what the teacher was saying or doing. This required a shift for me from a focus on teacher questioning to student thinking.

Carnegie Academy for the Scholarship of Teaching and Learning (CASTL). As a participant in the CASTL summer experiences, I joined a community of scholars who were examining their own teaching practices and students' learning (Hutchings 2000). We met in small groups to plan studies in our courses, to discuss data we had already collected, and to share drafts of our writings. Inspired by Lee Shulman's vision of instructors' communicating their "wisdom of practice" (2004), these sessions were pivotal for me, watching the Carnegie staff coaching college faculty who were new to the process and as unsure of themselves in this setting as teachers new to my inquiry groups, reading and discussing relevant literature, making progress on my own writing, and beginning to assemble a website documenting my teaching and my students' learning. The Carnegie Foundation for the Advancement of Teaching has developed software that teachers and college faculty can use to create websites that represent a study, a course transformation, course portfolio, or anatomy of a single class (see *www.cfkeep.org/static/index.html*). Known as the KEEP Toolkit (Tools for Knowledge, Exchange, Exhibition, and Presentation), the software is free and relatively straightforward to use. The Carnegie Foundation also has assembled documentary websites (called "snapshots of practice") in a Gallery of Teaching and Learning (see *http://gallery.carnegiefoundation.org*). I have documented how I used these websites in my course on methods of teaching in my own website at *www.cfkeep.org/html/snapshot.php?id=25417632* and in several papers (van Zee 2005b; van Zee and Roberts 2006). An exhibition of science-related documentary websites, including those by Claire Bove and Ellen Franz, can be viewed at *www.cfkeep.org/html/snapshot.php?id=88988139749494*. Through this national network of teachers interested in teacher research, we learned about Matt Ronfeldt's study of evolving ethical perspectives in his eighth-grade science classroom.

Looking at Data Seminars. While at the University of Maryland, I designed a course entitled "Studying Student Learning in Diverse Settings" for the Master's in Teacher Leadership program (Valli et al. 2006). Mary Bell, Kathleen Hogan, Trisha Kagey Boswell, and Elizabeth Kline were participants in this program. The main event for each session of my course involved participants in looking at data from their classrooms using guidelines from materials produced by the National Board for Professional Teaching Standards (*www.nbpts.org*). Over a series of four sessions, each participant in each small group of four presented and discussed with colleagues a set of student work (beginning of the course), a videotape of students in action (middle of the course), and an article interpreting these data (near the end of the course). These participants were free to ask their questions in any pedagogical context, not just science teaching and learning. Now at Oregon State University, I have initiated a "Looking at Data" seminar for graduate students, who bring in and discuss with their colleagues a wide variety of data from their master's and doctoral dissertation projects. Opportunities for such collaboration seem essential to me now at many levels.

Collaborative Inquiries at National Meetings. The Spencer Foundation sponsored several conferences for its grantees at which several Science Inquiry Group participants and I had met other teachers and college faculty engaged in collaborative inquiries. These were very affirming experiences for all of us and made possible communication with similar groups elsewhere. This evolved into a joint session at an American Educational Research Association (AERA) annual meeting at which several groups came together, not to present findings but rather to inquire into the collaborative inquiry process. Instead of papers presented to a silent audience sitting in chairs lined up in rows, our session was very interactive. We moved the chairs into several concentric circles and distributed ourselves around the ring. After very brief presentations (under three minutes) of our individual studies, each of us facilitated a small-group discussion with participants sitting nearby. After the small groups reported their findings, the whole group discussed recommendations for collaborative inquiry, occasionally erupting into boisterous laughter, an unusual occurrence at this conference. This taught me the importance of fostering interaction at meetings and led me to propose and facilitate a series of "Looking at Data" workshops and collaborative inquiry sessions at AERA and the National Association for Research on Science Teaching (NARST) annual meetings. These activities have profoundly changed the nature of my experience of professional conferences from a feeling of isolation to a warm sense of community. Mary Bell, Claire Bove, Monica Hartman, Kathleen Hogan, Christopher Horne, Deborah Roberts, and Dorothy Simpson have participated in these activities for several years—contributing the voice of teachers to the conversation among educational researchers.

Teacher Researcher Day at NSTA National Conferences. Although affirming and productive, the Spencer Foundation conferences and AERA session did not include many teachers with a focus on science. Deborah Roberts and I decided that we wanted to bring together teachers and college faculty working in science contexts. As cochairs of the Ad Hoc Committee for Practitioner Researcher of NARST, we started planning for such a conference. The Spencer Foundation funded a project through NSTA and NARST that enabled us to organize Teacher Researcher Day at NSTA national conferences. We received the contribution by the four TEAM teachers (Judy Fix, Norma Fletcher, Dianne Johnson, and Janet Siulc) through the informal network initiated through this effort. At Teacher Researcher Day, we put together a full day of activities, including a poster session, panel or workshop, and breakout sessions in which individuals and groups discuss their studies. As one participant described his experiences:

> Teacher Researcher Day allowed me to stand in one room (literally), look around, and say, "Wow! Here's a group of individuals dedicated to teaching/learning. It doesn't get any better than this!" I felt as though it elevated what I do as an individual and lends credibility to me, the classroom teacher. We had a ballroom full of excited individuals talking about student thinking and what that thinking meant. [teacher researcher, NSTA national conference, April 2003]

Closing Thoughts

This has been a very personal account of my experiences in participating in the evolving cultural phenomena of teachers inquiring into their own teaching practices and students' learning (Cochran-Smith and Lytle 1990, 1999; Roth, forthcoming; Zeichner and Noffke 2001). In a recent issue of *Teacher Education Quarterly* devoted to action research, the editors, Barbara Levin and Sherri Merritt, identified five features common to the papers: choice, systematic data collection and reflection, support, discomfort during the process, and the participants' empowerment and transformation (2006, pp. 3–4). These capture my commitments and experiences—participants need to generate their own questions and ways to explore these systematically, ongoing support is crucial, the process is hard work and can raise difficult issues, but the outcomes? As one participant expressed the impact of her experiences: "Teacher research is what kept me from walking out the door—if it weren't for teacher research, I wouldn't still be teaching!"

Reflections

In Chapter 10, Chris describes that over years of doing teacher research he learned "to stop talking ... and listen to what the students have to say. Pay close attention to what they have to say. Then use that kind of understanding to change my instruction." Emily has taken a similar journey as she has shifted her role from traditional university instructor to a facilitator of collaborative inquiries by teachers. Each voice in this book is that of a teacher. But without Emily's support and encouragement, most of the inquiries in this book would never have been undertaken, and the findings would never have been written. Each chapter here is evidence of what she values. Her contribution has been to support, and encourage, and "to stop talking and listen" to what these teachers have to say.

References

Cochran-Smith, M., and S. Lytle. 1990. Research on teaching and teacher research: The issues that divide. *Educational Researcher* 19 (2): 2–11.

Cochran-Smith, M., and S. Lytle. 1999. The teacher research movement: A decade later. *Educational Researcher* 28 (7): 15–25.

diSessa, A. A., D. Hammer, B. Sherin, and T. Kolpakowski. 1991. Inventing graphing: Metarepresentational expertise in children. *Journal of Mathematical Behavior* 10 (2): 117–160.

Doris, E. 1991. *Doing what scientists do: Children learn to investigate their world.* Portsmouth, NH: Heinemann.

Franz, E. (this volume). 2007. Jonathan. In *Teacher Research: Stories of Learning and Growing.* eds. D. Roberts, C. Bove, and E. H. van Zee. Arlington, VA: NSTA Press.

Gallas, K. 1995. *Talking their way into science: Hearing children's questions and theories, responding with curricula.* New York: Teachers College Press.

Hammer, D., and E. H. van Zee. eds. 2006. *Seeing the science in children's thinking: Case studies of student inquiry in physical* science. Portsmouth, NH: Heinemann.

Hubbard, R. S., and B. M. Power. 1993. *The art of classroom inquiry: A handbook for teacher research.* Portsmouth, NH: Heinemann.

Hubbard, R. S., and B. M. Power. 1999. *Living the questions: A guide for teacher researchers.* York, ME: Stenhouse Publishers.

Hutchings, P. 2000. *Opening Lines: Approaches to the scholarship of teaching and learning.* Palo Alto, CA: Carnegie Foundation for the Advancement of Teaching.

Iwasyk, M. 1997. Kids questioning kids: "Experts" sharing. *Science and Children* 35(1): 42–46.

Kurose, A. 2000. Eyes on science: Asking questions about the Moon on the playground, in class, and at home. In *Inquiring into inquiry learning and teaching in science.* eds. J. Minstrell and E. van Zee, 139–147. Washington, DC: American Association for the Advancement of Science. Retrieved July 24, 2006, from *www.aaas.org/programs/education/about_ehr/pubs/inquiry.shtml*

Levin, B. B., and S. P. Merritt. 2006. Action research for teacher empowerment and transformation. *Teacher Education Quarterly* 33(3): 3–6.

McDermott, L. C. 1990. A perspective on teacher preparation in physics and other sciences: The need for special science courses for teachers. *American Journal of Physics* 58: 734–742.

McDermott, L. C. 1996. *Physics by inquiry.* New York: Wiley.

Minstrell, J. 1989. Teaching science for understanding. In *Toward the thinking curriculum: Current cognitive research. 1989 Yearbook of the Association for Supervision and Curriculum Development,* eds. L. B. Resnick and L. E. Klopfer, 131–149. Alexandria, VA: ASCD.

Minstrell, J. 2001. Facets of students' thinking: Designing to cross the gap from research to standards-based practice. In *Designing for science: Implications from everyday, classroom and professional settings,* eds. K. Crowley, C. D. Schunn, and T. Okada, 415–444. Mahwah, NJ: Lawrence Erlbaum.

National Research Council (NRC). 1996. *National Science Education Standards.* Washington, DC: National Academy Press.

Pearce, C. 1999. *Nurturing inquiry.* Portsmouth, NH: Heinemann.

Roberts, D. 1999. The sky's the limit: Parents and first-grade students observe the sky. *Science and Children* 37: 33–37.

Roth, K. 2007. Science teachers as researchers. In *Handbook of research on science education* eds. S. K. Abell and N. G. Lederman. Mahwah, NJ: Lawrence Erlbaum.

Saul, W., J. Reardon, C. Pearce, D. Dieckman, and D. Neutze. 2000. *Science workshop: Reading, writing, and thinking like a scientist,* 2nd ed. Portsmouth, NH: Heinemann.

Schoenfeld, A., B. White, and D. Zimmerlin, 1999. The M.A. and Credential in Science or Mathematics Education. Retrieved July 24, 2006 from *www-gse.berkeley.edu/program/CD/macsme_pages/report.html*

Shulman, L. S. 2004. *The wisdom of practice: Essays on teaching, learning, and learning to teach.* San Francisco: Jossey-Bass.

Simpson, D. 1997. Collaborative conversations: Strategies for engaging students in productive dialogues. *The Science Teacher* 64 (8): 40–43.

Valli, L., E. H. van Zee, P. Rennet-Ariev, J. Mikeska, P. Roy, and S. Catlett-Muhammad. 2006. Initiating and sustaining a culture of inquiry in a Teacher Leadership Program. *Teacher Education Quarterly* 33 (3): 97–114.

van Zee, E. H. 1998a. Fostering elementary teachers' research on their science teaching practices. *Journal of Teacher Education* 49: 245–254.

van Zee, E. H. 1998b. Preparing teachers as researchers in courses on methods of teaching science. *Journal of Research in Science Teaching* 35: 791–809.

van Zee, E. H. 2005a. Teaching science teaching through inquiry. In *Elementary science teacher education: International perspectives on contemporary issues and practice*, ed. K. Appleton, 239–257. Mahwah, NJ: Lawrence Erlbaum.

van Zee, E.H. 2005b. Using web-based "Snapshots of Practice" to explore science learning and teaching in a course for prospective teachers. *Issues in Teacher Education* 14 (1) 63–79.

van Zee, E. H., M. Iwasyk, A. Kurose, D. Simpson, and J. Wild. 2001. Student and teacher questioning during conversations about science. *Journal of Research in Science Teaching* 38: 159–190.

van Zee, E. H., D. Lay, and D. Roberts. 2003. Fostering collaborative inquiries by prospective and practicing elementary and middle school teachers. *Science Education* 87: 588–612.

van Zee, E. H., and D. Roberts. 2001. Using pedagogical inquiries as a basis for learning to teach: Prospective teachers' perceptions of positive science learning experiences. *Science Education* 85: 733–757.

van Zee, E. H., and D. Roberts. 2006. Making science teaching and learning visible through web-based "snapshots of practice." *Journal of Science Teacher Education* 4: 367–388.

van Zee, E. H., and J. Minstrell. 1997a. Reflective discourse: Developing shared understandings in a high school physics classroom. *International Journal of Science Education* 19: 209–228.

van Zee, E. H., and J. Minstrell. 1997b. Using questioning to guide student thinking. *The Journal of the Learning Sciences* 6: 229–271.

White, R., and R. Gunstone. 1992. *Probing understanding*. London: Falmer Press.

Wild, J. 2000. How does a teacher facilitate conceptual development in the intermediate classroom? In *Inquiring into inquiry learning and teaching in science,* eds. J. Minstrell and E. H. van Zee, 157–163. Washington, DC: American Association for the Advancement of Science. Retrieved July 24, 2006, from: *www.aaas.org/programs/education/about_ehr/pubs/inquiry.shtml*.

Zeichner, K., and S. Noffke. 2001. Practitioner research. In *Handbook of research on teaching,* ed. V. Richardson, 4th ed. 298–330. Washington, DC: American Educational Research Association.

Note: Page numbers in *italics* refer to tables or figures.

Gallas, Karen, xviii, 25
Grade 1
    line graph interpretation, 3–4,
        127
    motion study by, 2–6, 126–127
    visiting university classes,
        126–128
    writing sequential directions,
        2, 4–6
Grade 4, electric circuit
    investigation, 16–22, 141
Grade 5
    science writing project, 10–14
    water condensation study,
        25–33
Grade 8, exploring ethical/moral
    issues, 58–70
Guided inquiry. *See* Inquiry-based
    science learning

Hammer, David, 150
Hartman, Monica, 1, 24
Hogan, Kathleen Dillon, 1, 2, 8,
    135, 149, 150, 151
Horne, Christopher, 87, 100, 150,
    152
Howes, Elaine, xxi
Hughes, Langston, 40–41
Hydrologic cycle. *See* Water cycle

Inquiry-based science learning,
    100–101, 135
    allowing time for wonder, 101,
        105, 119–120
    classroom climate for, 120
    giving space for, 108
    lesson on the Moon, 102–104
    of physics, 17, 94–98
    positive attitudes about science
        from, 128
    powerful questions and, 120–121

procedural outline, *90*, 105
teacher's role in, 121
See also Questions
Iwasyk, Marletta, xvii–xviii, 17

Johnson, Dianne, 87, 116
Journal records
    of individual student behavior,
        48–51
    kept by students, 74–75, 86
    of students' words, 42
    See also Teacher research
        procedures

Kline, Elizabeth, 1, 10, 151
Kohlberg, Lawrence, 62, 67, 69n, 70

Lay, Diantha, 87, 110, 148
Layman, John, 124–126, 127, 135,
    149
Letter writing, by teachers to
    students, 79–81, 83
Levin, Barbara, 153
Line graphs
    student interpretation of, 3–4,
        127, 130
    in teachers' physics course, 129
Literacy learning, 1

Merritt, Sherri, 153
Microcomputer-based laboratories
    (MBLs), 124, 125–126, 133
Minstrell, Jim, vii–viii, xxii–xxiii, 146
Moon
    inquiry-based dialogue on,
        102–104
    students' book about, 10–14
Mother to Son (Hughes), 40–41
Motion
    standards demonstrated by, *7*
    study of, 2–8, 127, 129–130,
        131–133

Teacher Research